CAPE COD & THE ISLANDS

PORTRAITS OF AMERICA

CAPE COD & THE ISLANDS

ELEANOR BERMAN

CHARTWELL
BOOKS, INC.

A QUINTET BOOK

Published by Chartwell Books Inc.,
A Division of Book Sales Inc.,
110 Enterprise Avenue,
Secaucus, New Jersey 07094

ISBN 0-89009-881-6

This book was designed and produced by
Quintet Publishing Limited
6 Blundell Street, London N7
in association with Footnote
Productions Limited

Art Director Peter Bridgewater
Editor Sheila Rosenzweig
Photographer Ian Howes

Typeset in Great Britain by
Leaper & Gard Ltd., Bristol
Colour origination in Hong Kong by
Hong Kong Graphic Arts Company Limited,
Hong Kong
Printed in Hong Kong by Leefung-Asco
Printers Limited

To my children, who introduced me to
the pleasures of Cape Cod and the Islands.

Photography: Ian Howes; © 1985 Leonard Harris;
and © 1985 Peter Ralston.

CONTENTS

PART I
CAPE COD

INTRODUCTION

*T*HERE is a legend on Cape Cod that any visitors who get sand in their shoes will come back again. Since hundreds of miles of glorious beaches are one of the chief lures of this Massachusetts vacationland and its famous offshore islands of Nantucket and Martha's Vineyard, it's a safe bet that most people do wind up with sandy traces of their visit—and an equally safe assumption that most visitors who discover the beauty of these exceptional destinations want to return.

The "Cape," as it is fondly known to its countless admirers, together with its islands, offers some of America's most exceptional scenery, coupled with the heritage and charm of an area whose history dates back more than 350 years.

People tend to forget that it was in Provincetown on the tip of the Cape that the Pilgrims made their first landing in 1620, pausing long enough to give thanks and explore the area before they moved on to the more sheltered harbor at Plymouth. It was off the shores of Provincetown that the Mayflower Compact, the proclamation of freedom that was the forerunner of the Declaration of Independence, was signed.

And it was back to the Cape that early settlers came to settle in the 1630s in villages like Sandwich, Barnstable and Yarmouth, towns that still bear the unmistakable stamp of Colonial America on their shady lanes.

The simple and practical "Cape Cod" house built by early settlers spawned an architectural style that continues to be popular to this day. The windmills that ground the corn and powered the industries of the early Cape remain also as atmospheric reminders of the past, along with the lighthouses that were beacons to countless ships at sea.

From Cape and Island ports, clipper ships and whalers ventured forth to bring back untold wealth, reflected in the fine sea captains' homes that continue to grace these towns today. Later still, the unmatched scenery attracted artists and writers to the Cape, turning villages like Provincetown into cultural havens known throughout the world. Few shore areas have such a rich history to offer to visitors. It is easy to understand why more people come each year and why increasing numbers decide to take advantage of the mild climate to live on the Cape year round.

Despite the crowds in high season, however, there is still solitude for those who seek it, and the fragile natural beauty that brought tourists in the first place remains for all to see, particularly in the 50 miles of beaches and 27,000 acres of unspoiled landscape of the Cape Cod National Seashore established by President John F. Kennedy on the lower Cape in 1961.

'From Cape and Island ports,
clipper ships and whalers ventured forth to
bring back untold wealth'.

A LAND CARVED BY GLACIERS

*T*HE Cape we see today is the remnant of an ancient coastline, a landscape carved by glaciers and still changing daily through the unceasing pressures of wind and water. Centuries ago, when the great glacier began to move beneath the pressure of its own weight, it ground its way southward from Labrador to cover more than half of North America, molding the face of the continent. Nowhere is its imprint seen more clearly than on the shore lands, which were creations of the last great Ice Age.

Eons before the glacier, the land of the Cape was covered with forests and grassy plains where dinosaurs roamed. Later the seas drowned the forests and covered them with mud and clay. New growth followed, and camels and horses soon grazed on the new marshy plains.

Then, 30,000 years ago, the glacier began to move through New England, taking with it mountain peaks and hilltops and leaving widening valleys in its wake. It dug into the earth, prying loose boulders and grinding them up in a mill of moving ice as it passed over them. When the march was slowed by currents of warm air near the coast, the glacier simply dropped its cargo of rocks and pebbles. These piles of once-solid bedrock formed ridges hundreds of feet high known as moraines. Such glacial rockpiles are the present hills of Nantucket and Martha's Vineyard and the spines of the Cape. One runs north and south along Buzzards Bay; another follows the shore of Cape Cod Bay from Sagamore to Orleans, then turns south to Chatham. Soil and trees and grass have coated the hills over the centuries, but only a few minutes of digging is necessary to come to the core of gravelly glacial material underneath.

Sometimes the ice failed to digest its rocky burden, dropping whole boulders which can still be seen on the Cape, particularly in the Falmouth–Woods Hole Area. Enos Rock in Eastham is the largest of these boulders, weighing thousands of pounds.

More signs of the glacier are evident to the keen eye almost everywhere. During periods when the ice retreated, the ocean rose and beds of blue clay formed in the sea, accounting for such areas as the cliffs known as the Clay Pounds of Truro, just north of Cape Cod Light. When the warming sun sent rivulets of water cascading from the glacier carrying rock and gravel, broad plains were built that are the present moors of Nantucket, the Great Plains of the Vineyard and the Cape's grassy "South Sea." Slow-melting ice-chunks left rounded pockets, the kettle holes that now dot the Cape landscape with more than 400 varying sized ponds.

At the end of the Ice Age some 10,000 years ago, the Cape was a barren bank marked by boulders and pocked with kettle holes. It was wider than it is today and ended at Truro highlands. Then seeds sprouted, reforesting and replanting the interior. And the sea began its work. The waters of the ocean rose, fed by melting ice, filling bays and flooding low-lying plains. Waves ground over gravel banks, continually carrying away rocks and stones in the tide, then returning them to shore worn down to smooth pebbles and sand. The relentless ocean eventually created wide borders of sand beach, rearranged harbors and bays, turned bars into spits and spits into peninsulas. Shoals grew into islands and islands became sheltering barrier beaches protecting placid bays.

Glacial debris was rearranged to build the hooked arm of Provincetown, much of Nauset Beach and all of Monomoy. Nantucket's Coatue Beach is recent in geologic time, as is the great South Beach on Martha's Vineyard.

With the new additions, there were also losses. Any Cape oldtimer can tell you tales of lost islands, such as Nauset Island off Eastham, once mapped by Champlain, now drowned under ocean water. Billingsgate Island, where Wellfleet farmers once pastured horses, is now a sandbar visible only at low tide.

Wind and water—that team of tireless sculptors—continue to carve new contours, reshaping shores, chipping at cliffs, building great sand dune piles that shift from moment to moment, constantly creating new hills and valleys in place of old.

Man, who did his own share to destroy the Cape's ecology through carelessness and overdevelopment, now does his best to stem the tides and slow the winds with breakwaters and beach grass. But, as has been true throughout the ages, it is nature that mended the first damage and that same inexorable nature that continues to create the changing face of the Cape.

Opposite and previous page The Cape Cod National Seashore established by President John F. Kennedy in 1961 preserved 50 miles of beach and 27,000 acres of unspoiled wetlands along one of America's loveliest shores.

EARLY DAYS ON THE CAPE

*T*HE first people to discover Cape Cod were the explorers seeking furs, gold, spices or whatever else could be found to bring them wealth. Though many believe the Vikings landed on Cape shores, there are no definite records of early explorers until the year 1602, when one Bartholomew Gosnold, an Englishman seeking gold, anchored near Provincetown and was so delighted with the numbers of codfish in the waters around his ship that he gave the Cape the name it has borne ever since.

Gosnold was followed in 1605 by French explorer Samuel Champlain, who gave French names to Provincetown and Wellfleet, Cap Blanc and St. Suzanne de Cap Blanc, before he ran out of provisions. Champlain and his party returned the next year to take a better look around, this time running into trouble with their boat near Chatham. The local Indians, who helped the newcomers repair the boat, were not so cordial when it looked as though they might have permanent neighbors, and the French fled, naming the spot Port Fortune because of their ill fortune there.

Captain John Smith, the next to arrive in 1614, mapped the coast and marveled over its abundant fish and game, feeling sure that gold and copper must be present somewhere in that land of plenty.

The First Settlers

It was not treasure but hope for a better life and freedom to practise their religion that took the Pilgrims on the long hard Mayflower voyage that brought them to Provincetown on November 11, 1620. Fighting the bitter cold of the season, they explored Truro and Wellfleet before landing permanently in the more sheltered waters of Plymouth.

When the new settlers arrived in Provincetown, they saw a shore that appeared to be a virgin wilderness, but they were actually in an organized community. Thirty-thousand Wampanoag Indians occupied the lands of the Cape and its two offshore islands in well-developed settlements that contained wooden houses as well as tepees. The 30 tribes of the Wampanoags had different names and leaders, but were loosely banded together under the leadership of a council of chiefs and their Supreme Sachem, Massasoit.

Despite their unwelcome reception to Champlain, the Cape Indians were amazingly friendly to the English newcomers to their lands. Early explorers had paved the way for the Pilgrims without knowing it by carrying some of the Wampanoags back to England with them. The Indian Squanto, who lived on the continent for two years and served as a guide, returned home familiar with English and the ways of white men. He accompanied Massasoit when the great Sachem paid a call on the new settlers at Plymouth, and he helped interpret a peace treaty between the Pilgrims and the Indians that lasted for 50 years. Squanto stayed with the Pilgrims, teaching them to fish and plant corn and acting as a guide and interpreter. Fewer

A bronze plaque set into a stone **right** marks the spot on Provincetown's First Encounter Beach where the Pilgrims first set foot on American soil. The date was November 21, 1620.

A replica of the Mayflower **opposite** stands near Plymouth Rock. Manned with costumed crew and passengers, it gives some notion of the ordeal of 102 brave souls who crossed the Atlantic in a 104-foot boat.

12

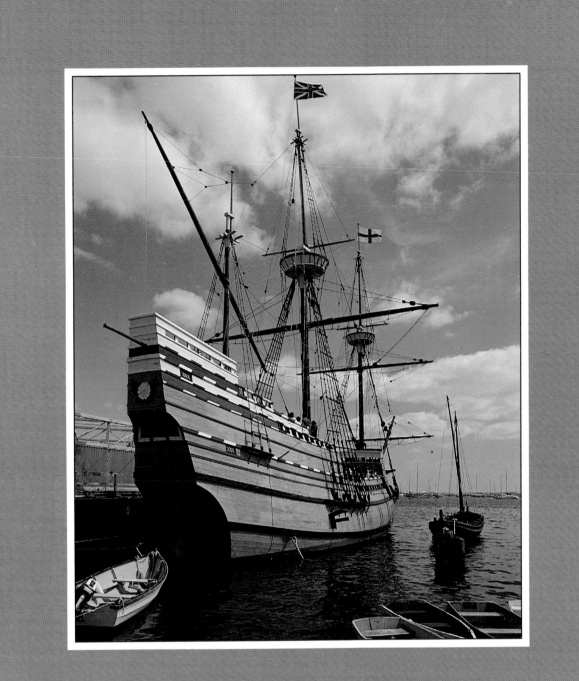

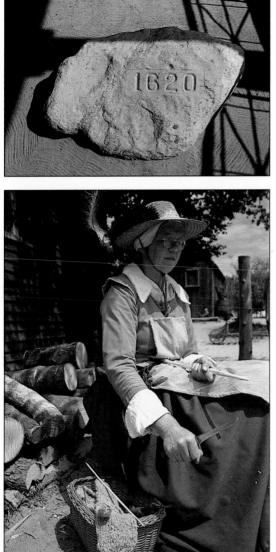

than half of the 102 Mayflower passengers survived that first winter. Without the aid of the Wampanoags, it is doubtful that any would have made it through.

Though it was a bountiful source of corn, Cape Cod was a nuisance to the first settlers because it blocked the water route allowing them to travel easily to New York and Connecticut to trade with the Dutch. The problem was solved in 1627. A trade route was established on the upper Cape at Scusset Creek and Monument River. The Manomet Trading Post came into being in what is now the town of Bourne, and travel to and from New York increased because the waterways allowed merchants to pass across the Cape rather than having to go around the peninsula.

The First Town

William Bradford, the first Governor of the Plymouth Colony, was also given a patent annexing the whole Cape to Plymouth County, and when settlers began grumbling about lack of space and the problem of insufficient fodder for their cattle, the Cape seemed the logical answer. In 1637, Edmund Freeman of Lynn led a band of ten to the neck of the Cape with orders to clear enough land for 60 families, and so Sandwich, the first Cape Cod community, was born. It was a fortunate site, close to the Manomet Trading Post, with plenty of salt marshes to provide hay for cattle fodder, plenty of herring to fertilize the farms and plenty of water to power a mill. The town was incorporated and officially named in 1639. Its citizens said quite frankly they had come "to worship God and to make money."

One ticklish question in the new town was how to divide the land fairly. The Plymouth court dispatched Captain Myles Standish to arrange matters in an equitable fashion, and with the assistance of John Alden, he did just that.

In that same year, Yarmouth was settled. Two of its first four residents were among

Scouting parties sailing out from Provincetown decided on the more sheltered harbor at Plymouth, just up the Massachusetts coast from Cape Cod, for their permanent settlement. It was here that much of the future of the Cape and the nation began. Their December 1620 landing spot is marked with a monument at Plymouth Rock **opposite** and the rock itself **above**.

At Plymouth Plantation a realistic replica of the rough village that existed here in 1627 is peopled with 'residents' trained to take the roles of the actual Pilgrims who established the first surviving colony in New England, with accuracy that extends even to their original native accents. Visitors find them at their daily chores — knitting needle **middle**, a blacksmith forging nails **below**.

Evidence of early times abound ... **opposite**, the village pump at Yarmouth. A wood-chopper **right** learns what it was like to carve a new life in the wilderness. Plymouth's realistic Pilgrims can answer any questions about their past life or their present existence — as long as the query doesn't concern anything after the early seventeenth century!

Sugar Maple The tree that is tapped for maple syrup. Native to the East it has winged 'samara' fruits which are dispersed by the wind.

the Mayflower pilgrims, though one eventually returned to Plymouth. Yarmouth's founders were a diverse group, hailing from varied backgrounds and areas of the Bay Colony. Though they built homes around the mill pond, there was considerable dissension, particularly on how to apportion their land, and even after Myles Standish once again intervened to perform this thankless task, disagreement remained the rule.

Meanwhile, Barnstable was settled and prospered under the guidance of Reverend John Lothrup. Many of Lothrup's congregation in England had followed their nonconformist minister across the Atlantic and through a succession of towns in the Bay Colonies. The reason for the name of the new town is obvious to those who have seen the similarity of the shore front of its English counterpart.

Eastham, the last of the four first Cape towns, was the richest in Pilgrim blood. It was founded in 1644 by a group from Plymouth that comprised almost half that town's population. Complaining about Plymouth's depleted soil and lack of available lands, the group moved to the richer area

then known as Nauset over the protests of their neighbors, who feared their settlement would be fatally weakened. The name was officially changed to Eastham in 1651, though the old name is still used for the beach and the lighthouse.

These first four towns eventually split into more towns. Falmouth separated from Plymouth in 1686 and Dennis from Yarmouth in 1794. Orleans, originally part of Eastham, was incorporated as a town in 1797. Harwich and Brewster came into being as a result of growth within Barnstable. One by one, towns continued to divide off from their parents until the Cape was made up of the 15 towns we know today.

Quakers who moved into Sandwich and Barnstable were judged heretics, and were harassed, imprisoned and stripped of their holdings. The farm of Christopher Holder, who led the Society of Friends in secret worship, has been maintained in East Sandwich as a museum. The Quaker Meeting House remains there also, testament to the spirit that the Pilgrims could not repress. In the 1700s, many Quakers found a home on Nantucket, where they played a major role.

Right Eastham, one of the four original settlements on the Cape, where the huge jawbones of a whale frame the entrance to the Penniman House.

The first generations on the Cape were as constrained in their occupations as in their religious practices. Former city dwellers found they had to be farmers or starve. Good food was abundant, for besides the corn and beans and onions grown in the fields, there were clams and lobsters, abundant cod and herring so plentiful that they were spread on the land for fertilizer. Still, every family had to be self-sufficient, for there were no markets to buy food or clothing. Each household grew its own food. The men sheared the sheep, the women spun the wool and sewed it into garments. Everyone had some cattle and sheep, which were profitable and required no pasturage, since they were turned loose to graze at will, their ownership marked with brands just as western cattle are today.

The number of cattle meant that tanners and cobblers were in demand right away, but even these "specialists" first tended to their own crops in the growing season.

Fish and Ships

Fishing has always been part of the Cape Cod scene, and generations of sons have followed their fathers out to sea. At the beginning, however, though fish was a staple on everyone's menu, the early farmers had enough to keep them occupied and did not consider fishing for a livelihood. Nor were they skillful enough to make the most of the abundant schools of cod and mackerel offshore. In order to take advantage of the potential revenue the sea's bounty represented, early fishing rights were given to specialists. Thomas Huckins of Barnstable is one of the first recorded as a commercial fisherman.

As the soil grew less fertile with overuse, more men looked to the sea for a living, and fishing fleets frequently went out from the Cape to the Grand Banks of Nova Scotia, where they loaded their boats with cod that had first been salted and dried on the beaches. Harwich, Barnstable and Chatham were the center of fishing in the 1700s.

During the Revolution, the British fleet effectively ended the fishing industry. Afterwards, the rebuilt fleet tended to head for new and closer fishing grounds along the Labrador Coast, and with shorter voyages the salting process was done at home. Layers of cod laid out to dry in the sun were a common sight on Cape Cod beaches. Salt-making grew into a major Cape occupation.

Though many towns had fishing fleets, Provincetown with its many miles of available beaches emerged as the center of the fishing industry. It prospered even further when Georges Banks grew up as a new source of rich catches, a destination within easy reach of its harbors. Wellfleet and Truro also benefited from their proximity to this new fishing ground. Outfitters like the Union Wharf Company of Provincetown became major participants in the fishing industry, not only stocking the boats but also providing fishermen's families with food on credit while the man of the house was at sea.

After the Civil War, fishing became big business, and smaller ports could not compete

Above Clammers in Osterville and throughout the Cape still relish the plentiful and delicious shellfish that nourished the original native Indians as well as the area's first Pilgrim settlers.

Below Fish and ships have been part of the Cape Cod scene since its earliest days. The abundant cod and mackerel in surrounding seas provided food and a livelihood for many settlers in the 1700s.

19

Lighthouses that were once beacons for early seafarers today are favorite subjects for Cape Cod photographers. Nauset Lighthouse near Nauset Light Beach is one of the best known.

A contemporary engraving showing a whale being stripped of its blubber at sea.

with the larger fleets that grew up in Gloucester and Boston. But Provincetown remained in the running, and the influence of the Portuguese fishermen attracted to her boats can still be felt in the town.

The first Cape Codders to benefit from whales did not even have to venture out to sea. When dead whales washed up to sea, their blubber was quickly stripped by settlers who boiled it down into oil to light their lamps. It was only a matter of time until men began seeking the whales, first in small fleets near shore, then in excursions out to sea. Almost every Cape community had a few daring whalers, but Truro and Provincetown were the pioneers in mounting whaling expeditions and whaling was a major occupation in Wellfleet as well before the Revolutionary War. None of them were equal to Nantucket, which blossomed into the third largest town in Massachusetts and supplied much of the oil that lit the world's lamps. Whaling brought great wealth to the island.

With the growth of the fishing and whaling fleet came the need for shipbuilders. Shipyards mushroomed from Buzzards Bay to Provincetown, constructing sturdy and seaworthy brigs and schooners for both fleets. The industry was at its peak in the mid-1800s, dwindling eventually as the industries they supported waned.

Fishing harbors remain picturesque parts of every Cape Cod shore community, and the lighthouses that are a legacy of its seafaring days are among its most photographed landmarks. Highland Light, also known as Cape Cod Light, was the first lighthouse to be built in 1797 and was the most powerful on the New England coast. Nobska Light at Woods Hole, Chatham Light, Sandy Neck and Nauset Lighthouse near the Nauset Light Beach are among the best known.

Cape Cod Windmills

On land, corn was the principal crop on Cape Cod. In the earliest days, it was also the medium of exchange in a society where no one

had any money. Indeed, it was noted in 1675 that there was "not five hundred pounds in all Plymouth Colony." Growing corn was simple, and it could be exchanged for labor and goods, but getting the corn ground was a problem, since the only mill was in Plymouth. Building new mills was difficult because it required skills that few of the settlers possessed. However, the need was urgent and great effort was made to find men with the mechanical skill to construct a mill. Waterpowered mills went up on streams in Falmouth, Bourne, Sandwich, Barnstable, Yarmouth, Brewster, Eastham and Truro, and many of them were still operating in the 1800s. The Sandwich mill has been restored and still turns today for visitors. But the most picturesque early structures remaining on Cape Cod are its windmills.

Back in 1849 when Henry David Thoreau took a walking trip around Cape Cod, he wrote, "The most foreign and picturesque structures on the Cape, to an inlander ... are the windmills—gray-looking octagonal towers, with long timbers slanting to the ground in the rear, and these resting on a cartwheel by which their fans are turned round to face the wind ... They looked loose and slightly locomotive, like huge wounded birds, trailing a wing or a leg, and reminded me of pictures of the Netherlands."

These romantic structures, arms outstretched against the sky, are said to be the most photographed antiquities in New England. Their original purpose was purely practical, however: to grind corn for meal. Since rushing streams are in short supply, but open space and the ever-present wind are plentiful on Cape Cod, it was only natural that this readily available power source would be utilized. However, finding millwrights who could build these complex structures was even more difficult than finding those who could construct water wheels. The art of the millwright was second only to a shipbuilder in its complexity, and required some of the same know-how, since early windmills utilized sails to catch the wind. Men who had the ability were highly esteemed, and many towns offered special compensation to induce competent millwrights to move to their community.

The first contract for a windmill on Cape Cod is in the Barnstable Town records, dated 1687. It was built by the most celebrated of all Cape millwrights, Thomas Paine of Eastham.

The Old Mill on the Village Green in Eastham is a surviving original Colonial windmill and treasured landmark. Whirling sails on these slats once provided the power to turn millstones, thus grinding grain into the meal that was a mainstay for early Cape Cod households.

Paine traveled the length of the Cape to meet the demand for his services. His first two structures were put up for his fellow citizens in Eastham in 1683–84. Then he put up the first windmill in Barnstable and, not to be outdone, Yarmouth promptly ordered its own mill. When Paine went down to Truro to build a windmill, he liked it so much he settled in the town and became one of its leading citizens.

Soon every town on the Cape had its windmill, the number growing as the population increased. By 1800, a total of 39 windmills were spinning the length and breadth of Cape Cod, most of them the Dutch "smock" type resembling an octagonal tower covered with shingles, broader at the base and tapering slightly toward the top.

Second in prestige only to the millwright was the miller, who also needed mechanical ability to perform his job. Many millers were retired seamen, whose experience handling sails at sea enabled them to tend the canvas windmill sails, which were rigged in nautical fashion and required setting and furling just like the sails of a ship. The work was hard and dangerous and the miller had to be a shrewd caller of wind and weather to avert broken arms or other catastrophes. The tale is still repeated of the Dennis miller who forgot to make the mill arms fast before he went out to adjust his sail, sending himself for an unexpected spin.

Going to the mill was one of the few breaks in the hard-working farmer's routine, allowing time to exchange the news of the day while the corn was being ground.

Windmills also powered another major early occupation on Cape Cod, the making of salt. As has been noted, salt was an important commodity, not only for seasoning but also for curing fish, the Cape's most important product. England had put an exorbitant tax on imported salt, inspiring the Colonists to devise a way to make use of the salt water that surrounded them.

In 1776, a retired skipper named John Sears was the first to devise a way to use the sun's evaporating rays to produce salt, a project that earned the skeptical name of "Sears' Folly" when it was found that it took 350 gallons of hand-drawn water to make one bushel of salt. But Sears kept at it, and in 1785, he devised a pump that could be activated by the wind to make the process more efficient. Salt-making became an industry second only to shipmaking, and by the early 1880s, there were 136 operations on the Cape producing 40,000 bushels of salt a year. When the blockades of the War of 1812 made domestic salt even more valuable, the figure grew to 442 saltworks producing over half a million bushels a year and bringing great prosperity to the Cape. The industry declined after 1840, when imported salt became less expensive.

The Farris Mill, thought to be the oldest windmill in America, was moved from West Yarmouth to Dearborn, Michigan in the 1930s, but six of the old mills remain, and many still grind corn into meal during the summer months to the delight of visitors. Only The Old Mill on Nantucket remains on its original site. The surviving windmills on Cape Cod are The Old East Mill, which was moved from Orleans to Heritage Plantation in Sandwich; The Judah Baker Mill, removed from South Yarmouth to stand in a park at Bass River; The Brewster Windmill, relocated to a site adjacent to the Drummer Boy Museum on Route 6A in Brewster; The Old Mill in Chatham, moved to Rink Hill in Chase Park, and The Old Mill in Eastham on the Village Green across from the Eastham Town Hall.

More Cape Cod windmills may still be seen, transformed to a use their millwrights might never have anticipated, as quaint guesthouses or studios.

Miniature versions of Cape Cod's fascination with the wind can be seen in the form of toy windmills and whimsical whirligigs which are a local specialty and a favorite Cape Cod souvenir.

Early settlers might smile to see that in our age of technology, experiments are once again

attempting to harness the wind to produce energy that will reduce our dependence on oil as a fuel. The modern machines with slender metal blades mounted on lightweight steel towers bear little resemblance to the old-timers, but they can be seen on the Cape and the Islands as private companies use the plentiful breezes to test new ways to produce wind power. The major recent experimental centers are the Cycloturbine at New Seabury, the Energy Research Development Administration project on Nantucket and the New Alchemy Cape Cod Farm under the auspices of the New Alchemy Institute of Woods Hole.

The Cape Cod House

One of the most lasting contributions Cape Cod has made to the nation is the ingenious and practical design of the homes built by its early residents. The first recorded use of the term "Cape Cod house" is in the writing of Timothy Dwight. He traveled widely in New England in 1800, and recorded his impressions in letters, which noted the houses of the less wealthy inhabitants "generally of the class which may be called, with propriety, Cape Cod houses." Though others noted the distinctive homes from time to time, it was not until the Depression of the 1930s that the nation really began to appreciate the economical and intelligent design of these modest homes.

WEATHERVANES

Whimsical weathervanes are silhouetted against the sky on rooftops throughout the Cape. A dolphin in Chatham **left** , an eagle in Harwich **right** and the horse-drawn fire engine atop Brewster's Fire Museum **above** are among the prizes to be spotted. Many others include the famous gilded cock on the West Parish Church in West Barnstable and the rooster on the Saint Barnabas Memorial Church in Falmouth. Many forms exist: swordfish, a two-masted schooner, geese, even the ubiquitous cod.

This 1700s cottage in Eastham
is typical of the weathered gray saltbox
houses that abound on
Cape Cod, adding charm to a stroll on almost
any winding lane.

The "typical" Cape Cod house is one-and-a-half stories high with a steeply pitched roof. The homes were built low to the ground to ride out the winds and rains of the nor'easters that lash the Cape from time to time. "A short hoist and a long peak," was the builder's guiding motto.

The houses were firmly anchored to the ground by a good-sized chimney, which stood opposite the front door and rose through the ridge line of the roof. It was the chimney that gave the house its special charm and character, a central core that served several fireplaces and decided the location of the rooms and the placement and pitch of the stairs.

Long before the idea of solar homes came into being, Cape Cod houses were placed facing south, so that the low winter sun could add warmth. This was important, since fireplaces were the only source of heat in the home. The placement also was useful in telling time, since the family knew it was noontime when the sun shone directly in the front windows.

There are three basic kinds of homes that can still be seen all over the Cape today. The half-house has two windows on one side of the door, the three-quarter house has two windows to one side and one to the other and the full Cape, sometimes called a "double house," has a door in the center with two windows on either side. The styles could be enlarged and even made smaller. They were adapted according to the space needs of the owner, with quarter-houses sometimes added, full Capes sometimes created by joining two half-houses and two half-houses occasionally formed by dividing a whole house.

The basic floor plan was always the same for all of these styles. At the back of the house is a "keeping room," a large rectangular room with a low ceiling that served as kitchen, workshop and living area. Off the keeping room were two smaller rooms, the buttery, where food, dishes and household items were kept and the "borning room," literally the place where children were born and where infants could be placed in easy reach of their mothers. In remodeled Capes, the buttery often becomes a bath and the borning room is used as a small bedroom or den.

The front of the house contained the bedroom and the parlor. The latter was usually placed on the southeast corner to the right of the door to take best advantage of the sun's

Northern Mockingbird A natural mimic, the mockingbird with his tail flipping jauntily can be spotted in both the towns and the countryside.

Left The classic front door style of Daley Cottage was typical of Cape Cod houses in the 1700s. The cottage is open to the public.

warming rays. It was used only for formal occasions such as a wedding or funeral or minister's visit, and was the most elaborately finished and furnished room in the house.

As the family grew, more rooms could be added upstairs under the steep eaves. Because the early roofs had no dormers, the sleeping space in the attic depended on windows in the gable ends for light and ventilation, adding to the distinctive look of the homes.

After a walk up Nauset beach in 1849, Thoreau wrote:

Their garrets were apparently so full of chambers that their roofs could hardly lie down straight and we did not doubt that there was room for us there ... The great number of windows in the ends of the houses and their irregularity in size and position ... struck us agreeably, as if each of the various occupants who had their cunabula behind had punched a hole where his necessities required it, and according to his size and stature, without regard to outside effect. There were windows for the grown folks and windows for the children—three or four apiece; as a certain man had a large hole cut in his barn door for the cat and

One-and-a-half stories high to make the most of space, built low to the ground to ride out the winds and rains, the ingenious and practical early design that became known as the 'Cape Cod house' was widely adapted and is still used throughout the nation.
Right A modern dwelling built to the design.
Opposite A 1700s house in Orleans.

another smaller hole cut for the kitten.

Cape Cod houses are as charming to the eye today as when they caught the imagination of Thoreau, and they can be seen in every town, their weathered shingles polished shiny silver-gray from years of salt spray, wind and sun, their exteriors often adorned with rambler roses. Some of the special ones to watch for are the Captain Jonathan Kenrick House in East Dennis, the Saconesset Homestead, now a historical museum in West Falmouth, the Old Atwood House in Chatham, the home of the Chatham Historical Society and the Gregory House, believed to be the oldest house in Provincetown.

The salt-box house is less common on the Cape than in other sections of New England, but it appeared early and is evident in many towns, marked by its short front roof and long sloping back, a shape resembling the salt containers that inspired the name. Since Cape houses usually face south, the design proved practical, as the back roof took the brunt of winter storms from the north and winter snow slid easily to the ground. One of the oldest remaining salt-box homes is the Hoxie House in Sandwich, which has been dated at 1637.

Cape Cod architecture changed with the times. Two-story Colonial houses popular around Boston were emulated on the Cape. Sea captains' houses tended to replace a pitched roof with a hip roof, often called a "square rigger" and featured additional details such as cupolas and the fenced-in upper platform known as the "widow's walk," said to be named for its use by wives scanning the horizon for the return of their seafaring husbands. The Village Green in Falmouth is a fine spot for viewing the range of eighteenth-century styles.

In the next century, when fortunes were being made in whaling and trading, the homes became even finer. By mid-century, Greek Revival architecture had influenced Cape home design, particularly from Chatham to Provincetown, the Lower Cape, which was

Spacious Hyannis beaches **above** offer a commodious welcome to early summer visitors who arrive ahead of the mid-season crowds.

Wind surfers **below** are among the newest sights adding color to the coast off Hyannis, joining the sailors who have long found these to be prime sporting waters.

experiencing its greatest growth during this period. The Captain Bangs Hallet House in Yarmouthport is a fine example of the Greek Revival style. Though these later homes are different from the traditional Cape, they share its simplicity of design, a quality that remained until the flamboyant Victorian period.

The enduring Cape Cod home still remains for most people symbolic of the Cape, and has been rediscovered for compactness and beautiful proportions. The old "keeping room" has emerged to something like its original purpose in the modern family room. The sensibility of Cape Cod home design tells us much about the early settlers, who made the most of what they had to work with.

Cape Cod Today

Cape Cod has had many ups and downs through its long history. The British blockade all but ruined its fishing industry in the late 1700s and the War of 1812 was another blow to the sea trade that was the major livelihood of the Cape. Then commerce bloomed again as traders and whalers brought home wealth beyond anyone's dreams. In 1848, the railroad arrived, a boost to fishermen, cranberry growers and the makers of glass in Sandwich, all of whom could now bring their goods to market more easily. Then came the trauma of the Civil War, the close of the seafaring era, the demise of the Sandwich Glass Factory, the end of the salt-making industry.

Times were hard and many young residents began to seek their fortunes elsewhere. But just about the time they were leaving, the tourists began to arrive. There were inn-keepers on the Cape as early as the 1600s, but never did they foresee that their occupation was to become a new major industry on Cape Cod. The forward-looking wealthy began building summer homes around Falmouth and Hyannis in the 1870s, and it was only a matter of time before all the Cape towns were discovered by everyone who values beach and beauty. Tourism saved the Cape, though many now worry that it will ruin the treasure it uncovered.

Sandwich glass This jar was decorated by the famous Mary Gregory. Many more examples are displayed in the Sandwich Glass Museum.

People commonly speak of the 70-mile length of the Cape today as if it were one community, but to a native it is a series of subdivisions as pronounced as though there were high walls dividing the parts. The shape of Cape Cod has been aptly compared to a flexed arm, with the Upper Portion or shoulder the westernmost section that includes the disparate towns of Sandwich, Bourne, Falmouth and Mashpee. The Mid-Cape is made up of the towns of Barnstable, Yarmouth, Dennis, Brewster and Harwich, each further divided into many villages. And the narrow Lower or Outer Cape begins at the elbow at Chatham and continues through Orleans, Eastham, Wellfleet and Truro to Provincetown, the clenched fist at the end.

The divisions are more than geographical, for each part of the Cape has a distinct personality. The Upper Cape, with the Cape Cod Canal, the rapidly growing town of Falmouth, Otis Air Force Base, the Woods Hole Research community and the Massachusetts Maritime Academy, has a flavor that is repeated nowhere else. The job opportunities, along with its proximity to Boston, have contributed to rapid year-round growth.

The Mid-Cape, including bustling Hyannis, is the most populous region with the best warm water beaches; it bears the greatest brunt of summer tourist crowds. The Lower Cape is the last bastion of endless Atlantic Ocean beach and wide-open spaces, mainly because of the National Seashore.

Before it makes its elbow turn at Chatham, the wider Upper and Mid-Cape are also divided into two sides, the North facing Cape Cod Bay and the South facing Nantucket Sound. The two sides have their own differences. The South side running along Route 28 has warmer water and better beaches, while the North has retained more of its original Early American look, particularly along its main route, 6A, the Old Kings Highway that has been declared an historical district all the way from Sandwich to Orleans. The importance of this district can easily be seen by comparing the road to the commercial overgrowth across the peninsula on Route 28.

From Chatham to Provincetown, the Cape narrows considerably, becoming as little as a mile wide in some areas. Each section has its special assets and attractions that warrant a closer look.

THE UPPER CAPE

The four Upper Cape towns are neighbors, but they are completely different from each other and from the rest of the area. The growing population is a fascinating mix of descendants of the earliest settlers, including the Wampanoags, and increasing numbers of those who "got sand in their shoes"—the summer people who came back to stay. With Boston only a 60-minute bus ride away, the commuter parking lot by the Sagamore Bridge has been expanded twice in less than a decade. Retirees are also contributing to an explosion that has tripled the size of Sandwich and Mashpee and boosted Falmouth to a town of 25,000 year round, with more than twice that number in the summer.

Parts of the Upper Cape are the heart of the cranberry industry, with bogs a prominent feature around Bourne and Mashpee. Falmouth's kettle ponds, Bourne's boulders, the Mashpee River and the Sandwich ridge were created by the great glacier, but the most prominent part of the Upper Cape landscape is manmade.

The Cape Cod Canal

When the Cape Cod Canal opened in 1914, it was the culmination of an idea that had been under discussion for 250 years. Myles Standish and George Washington were among many who noted that less than a mile lay between the Manomet and Scusset Rivers, but though the first committee was appointed to study the matter back in 1697, it was not until the late 1800s that serious plans were laid. Even then the first attempt ended with bankruptcy, and it was only with the backing of financier August Belmont that the final project got started with the scooping of the first shovel of dirt broken by a silver spade in 1909.

Belmont thought the project would make him even richer, but when the canal was sold to the government eventually, his estate wound up losing money. Both Bourne and Sandwich expected to become centers for heavy shipping, but by the time the canal was finished, so was heavy industry on the Cape.

The canal made the Cape an island cut off from the mainland, but it also made it far more easily accessible over its bridges. Today the canal is a waterway for pleasure boats, tankers and tugs and a scenic welcome for visitors crossing the Bourne or the Sagamore Bridge.

Sandwich

The oldest town on the Cape is one of its loveliest. Though it was an industrial town for much of the nineteenth century, Sandwich center is possibly the most perfectly preserved colonial enclave remaining on Cape Cod.

It is a village of wide lawns, gracious homes and spired New England churches, with a Town Hall dating back to 1837. Nine buildings in the historical district date from the seventeenth century, and 14 were built in the eighteenth century. The Dexter Grist Mill on Shawme Pond near the center of town is a restoration of the Mill that operated here in 1640. Next door is the Hoxie House, one of the oldest homes on the Cape. The 1638 First Parish Meetinghouse currently houses a doll museum, and the First Church of Christ boasts what is said to be the oldest church bell in America in its Christopher Wren steeple, dating back to 1675. Though the present building is a reconstruction following a fire, the Daniel Webster Inn has origins dating back to 1692, making it one of the nation's oldest hostelries.

Next to the mill is the Thornton Burgess Museum, dedicated to the author of the Peter Rabbit stories, who grew up in Sandwich. Web-footed creatures of all kinds stroll the lawns here, adding to the charm of the setting.

One of the best known attractions in town is the Sandwich Glass Museum, where several rooms handsomely display a comprehensive collection of the renowned glassware that was made here from 1825 to 1888. The instantly recognizable "lacy" patterns developed here continue to influence glassware design, and the glowing colors produced in the middle of the last century are as stunning today as they were when they were created.

Passing the canal toll.

Many-hued Cape Cod sunsets such as this one **opposite** at Monument Beach have served as inspiration for countless artists and photographers as well as those content **34** just to bask in the beauty.

SHAWME POND MILL

The mill wheel still turns
on Shawme Pond in Sandwich. The
restoration of the original
mill built here by Thomas Dexter before 1654
demonstrates just how
the old mills ground the cornmeal that was a
main ingredient of early
Colonial recipes. Visitors can buy the freshly
ground meal for their own
use.

The Sandwich Historical Society's Glass Museum **above** displays the finest creations of the renowned Boston and Sandwich Glass Company founded in 1825 by Deming Jarves, who determined to produce fine glass that was affordable. The factory operated for 63 years, beginning with blown glass and then pioneering in the development of pressed glass, particularly the 'lacy' glass that originated here. Some of the worlds' finest glassblowers worked in Sandwich, producing masterpieces in glowing colors.

Fishing boats off the Cape Cod shore near Sandwich harbor **below**. Though best known for its perfectly preserved Colonial center, Sandwich has the fifth-largest fishing fleet in Massachusetts.

Sandwich Plantation, a more recent addition, once the private estate of horticulturalist Charles Dexter, is a 76-acre showplace of prize rhododendron gardens and a complex of museums built to house the private collections of Josiah K. Lilly, Jr. Antique cars, guns, military memorabilia and miniatures, paintings, folk art and one of the largest collections of Currier and Ives photographs to be found are housed here in unique buildings, such as a round barn inspired by the Shaker barn in Hancock, Massachusetts and a reproduction of a Revoutionary War period structure in New Windsor, New York. An old Orleans windmill has been moved here and there is a real old-fashioned 1912 carousel still in perfect order, offering visitors a nostalgic ride.

Though it is not one of the better beach towns on the Cape, Sandwich does offer some particularly fine nature preserves.

Falmouth

With 55 miles of shoreline and 12 miles of public beaches, Falmouth is generally con-

The 1800 windmill at Heritage Plantation **right** was moved from Orleans, where it ground meal for residents for 93 years. With new help from a motor, it still grinds corn for visitors.

Staghorn Sumak This tree which is found in the northeast is noted for its brilliant fall foliage and its crimson lollipop fruits.

who wanted to escape the repression taking place in Sandwich and Barnstable. West Falmouth remained a Quaker stronghold until the Civil War, and their meetinghouse still stands on Route 28A. The restored 1756 Congregational Church facing the Village Green has a bell cast by Paul Revere. Two of the historic homes on the Green, the 1790 Julia Wood House and the 1740 Conant House, are now the museums of the Falmouth Historical Society, full of relics of its early days. Another local historic spot is the Katherine Lee Bates House, where the author of "America the Beautiful" was born.

Not all of the reminders of the past are in museums. Falmouth was one of the few Cape communities attacked by the British during the Revolutionary War, and was a target again during the war of 1812 when the British sailed in and demanded that the town's cannons be turned over to them. The stalwart citizens refused, prompting shelling from the harbor. The Elm Arch Inn and the Nimrod Inn still display their battle scars.

In the 1800s, Falmouth was a shipbuilding and whaling center, and the fine homes of the ships' captains still grace the town. It was also a fishing and salt-making center and prime ground for cranberry and strawberry growers in its early years. In the middle of the 1800s, it was one of the first to attract summer visitors to the Cape when millionaire Joseph Storey Fay foresaw the future of Woods Hole as a resort and bought up many acres, prompting many wealthy Bostonians to follow. The sea captains objected to seeing their town change, but early summer residents like the Fays, Beebees and Lillys have been generous to Falmouth, donating churches, recreational facilities and parks.

Some of the sights of the area are the Waquoit Congregational Church, old homes and views of the bay in Waquoit, the 1797 East End Meeting House on Sandwich Road in East Falmouth, the drive along Shore Road from East Falmouth into town, and the water views from the "Great Hill" in Falmouth Heights where Queen Awashonks, a Wampanoag ruler, used to summer. Silver Beach is a handsome area of old summer homes, and Hatchville is best known as the home of the Falmouth Playhouse, one of the oldest and best of the many excellent summer theatres on the Cape.

sidered the nautical and tourist center for the Upper Cape. It has the biggest downtown area on the Upper Cape, but despite its build-up in recent years, it remains an area of great natural beauty with several wildlife refuges and a botanical garden maintained by the Massachusetts Audubon Society.

Today's Falmouth is made up of many hamlets such as Waquoit, Teaticket, Smalltown, Hatchville, Mara Vista, Quissett, Sippewisset, Silver Beach and Megansett, not to mention North, East and West Falmouth.

The village of Woods Hole is also technically part of Falmouth, adding a scientific accent to the community with its world-renowned Oceanographic Institute and the Northeast Fishery Center of the National Marine Fishery Service. The harbors here bustle with research vessels as well as Coast Guard cutters and the comings and goings of the Nantucket and Martha's Vineyard ferries.

Falmouth has a long and full history. It has the distinction of being the first place that Englishmen landed in the New World when Bartholomew Gosnold cast anchor here in 1602. Some of its first settlers were Quakers

With flags by day and beacons
at night, Nobska Lighthouse **above** has
stood on her rocky perch
above one of the Cape's busiest channels
since 1828, guiding seamen
past treacherous shoals to safe berths in
Little Harbor and Great
Harbor at Woods Hole. The present
lighthouse was constructed
in 1878.

One of the two impressive Colonial homes of the Falmouth Historical Society on the village green **right**, containing portraits, toys, kitchen utensils, whaling items, scrimshaw, silver, glass, china and many other mementos of the town's past.

Bourne

Bourne is both the oldest and youngest town on the Cape. It was originally part of Sandwich, the first settlement, and in 1884 was the last of the towns to be separately incorporated.

Though Bourne emerged with the warm-water coast and the eventual canal site, Sandwich retained fishing and shell-fishing rights which have been a source of contention between the towns ever since.

Long before white settlers came, tribes of the Wampanoag Federation lived in Bourne. There were two prominent Bournes in Cape history, Richard Bourne of Sandwich, the early leader whose mission was the conversion of the Indians to Christianity, and Johnathan Bourne, a prosperous whaling merchant. The first trading post on the banks of the Manomet River was also in the present village of Bourne,

and a reproduction of that Aptucxet Trading Post has been built on the original site. Like Sandwich, Bourne was rural in its early days and became industrialized in the 1800s. Its mills, comb and button factory, lumbering and turpentine industries spurred the development of railroads into the Cape, and the railroad brought more summer people into the area.

Bourne's principal sights are its fine summer homes and ocean views in villages such as Cataumet and Pocasset. Sagamore is also part of Bourne. It is a town that was divided by the Cape Cod Canal; part of it lies across the bridge. Many Italian workers brought in to work on the bridge in the 1800s settled here, giving a unique flavor to the town.

Bourne's main shopping area is Buzzards Bay, home of the Massachusetts Maritime Academy, which prepares young men and women for the Merchant Marine. The area's first railroad bridge came into Buzzards Bay in 1848, a welcome addition to the makers of the fine glassware that was the trademark of Sandwich at that time.

Graceful Bourne Bridge **above**, built in the 1930s, spans the southern end of the Cape Cod Canal. It is the scenic gateway to the Cape for thousands of visitors each year.

When the first railroad bridge came into Buzzard's Bay in 1848, it was a boon to tourism and to the burgeoning glass-manufacturing business on the upper Cape. The Bourne Railroad Bridge shown here **below** was built after the creation of the Cape Cod Canal. It took two years to build and cost almost $2 million, yet ironically, with the growth of automobile travel it now carries only a few freight trains each week.

Long before the Pilgrims arrived on Cape Cod, the Massipee tribe of the Wampanoags was living, farming and fishing in the area that now comprises Mashpee. Threatened by new diseases brought by the white man, deprived of their lands, the Massipees were in need of aid, and Richard Bourne of Sandwich was one who attempted to help them by teaching them Christianity and the English language. Bourne, who was ordained minister of the "Praying Indians," was instrumental in helping the

Mashpee's Old Indian Meeting House **opposite**, Cape Cod's oldest church building, was built in 1684 on Briant's Neck, then moved to its present site in 1717. Richard Bourne, a Sandwich missionary who befriended the Wampanoags and converted many to Christianity, was pastor here and was instrumental in having the church built. It was completely restored and rededicated in 1970.

The annual herring run in Mashpee **left** brings thousands of fish upstream, fighting their way against the current aided by fish ladders to spawn in the same waters where they were born.

Indian obtain title to the Plantation of Mashpee. The fate of the tribe has not always been a happy one, but Mashpee remains a rare example of the blend on the Cape between its original inhabitants and the newcomers who shared and often took their lands.

The Wampanoag Indian Museum, Old Indian Meeting House and Mashpee burial grounds are all reminders of the town's Indian heritage.

Present-day Mashpee has a considerable amount of manufacturing, helping to provide employment for its Indian population. It is also a town of fine beaches, with some 26 miles of ocean frontage. The recent large New Seabury resort development has caused concern, and the town has supported efforts to preserve its natural attractions with a River Scenic Act in 1980 to protect the placid freshwaters of the Mashpee River. An act passed in 1981 allowed the state to take the 432 acres of South Cape Beach in order to shelter its saltwater marshes, pine woods and the unspoiled beaches.

Mashpee is unique for its spring herring run. Each spring, thousands of fish swim up the Mashpee River to fight their way against the current, up ladders to the pond above and to Mashpee Lake, where they spawn. Their young make their way back to the sea, eventually to return also to spawn in the waters where they were born.

THE MIDDLE CAPE

The best and worst of Cape Cod can be found in its center—some of the best warm water beaches, some of the finest early architecture, some of the biggest summer traffic jams.

The area is made up of several towns: Barnstable, Yarmouth, Dennis, Harwich and Brewster, and most of them are further subdivided into many villages. Among the "villages" of Barnstable is Hyannis, the hub of the Mid-Cape and its shopping center. As the seat of Barnstable County, which encompasses the entire Cape, Barnstable is the political center of the area.

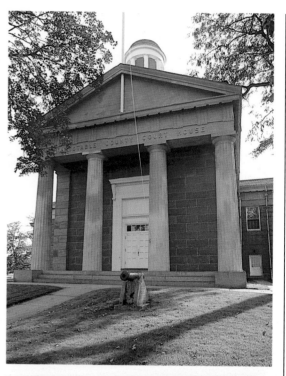

Barnstable

The original Barnstable settlement under the leadership of Reverend John Lothrop was on the North shore near the great salt marshes. Other ministers and their congregants followed to escape the repression in Plymouth and other Bay colonies. Farming, whaling and fishing supported these early communities, and in the 1800s Barnstable supplied many of the ship captains who guided American clipper ships on the high seas. Many of their homes remain along the beautifully preserved Old Kings Highway, Route 6A.

Today's Barnstable also retains many other interesting reminders of the past, including the West Parish Meeting House built by Lothrop's followers. The church bell was made by Paul Revere and donated by patriot James Otis, a Barnstable native son. Lothrop's second home also still stands as part of the Sturgis Library on Route 6A, the oldest public library in the United States. The Olde Court House is nearby, as is the Barnstable Village Hall, now home to the Barnstable Comedy Club, founded in 1922 as one of the country's first community theater groups. Its alumni include Kurt Vonnegut.

The Crocker Tavern in the middle of the village, built in 1754 to house stagecoach travelers, is now open to the public. Another historic

A contemporary engraving of a ship's crew in the early 1900s.

The Olde Colonial Court House **above** is filled with mementos of the eventful early history of Barnstable. The cannons out front guarded the town during the War of 1812. The building is still in active use as a court house, as it has been since 1832.

Barnstable's West Parish Meeting House **below**, built by the followers of founder Reverend John Northrop, dates back to 1639. Through its front door **opposite** later passed patriots like native son James Otis, who donated the Paul Revere church bell in the steeple.

S A N D Y   N E C K

Sandy Neck, with its tall dunes, cranberry
bogs and a six-mile barrier beach, is the most
extensive conservation area outside of the
National Seashore and the largest salt marsh
complex on the Cape. It offers swimming, surf
casting and other recreation as well as open
spaces and a quiet retreat for both wildlife
and visitors in search of tranquility. The
upland is available for hiking and horseback
riding.

site, the Custom House atop Cobb's Hill, marks the period beginning in 1789 when the village was headquarters for a custom district and an entry port for foreign ships. This 1856 building, transformed into a museum of Colonial and Indian life can also be visited.

A feature of current Cape life is Barnstable's Cape Cod Art Association Gallery displaying work by local artists.

Hyannis

Though technically part of Barnstable, Hyannis and Hyannis Port deserve special mention since, thanks to the Kennedy family, they have become the places most people immediately associate with the Cape. Busy Hyannis is the Cape's shopping and transportation cross-roads, a rapidly growing community that is a terminal for buses, planes and boats to the islands, as well as the scene of much of the nightlife on the Cape, including the famous Melody Tent where many Broadway stars have performed. Cape Cod Mall with some six dozen stores is by far the most extensive shopping area to be found in the region, and it is only the start of what is available in Hyannis: skating rinks, arcades, restaurants, golf, tennis, bikes, canoes and just about any kind of recreation that might please a tourist. It is estimated that some six million visitors take advantage of Hyannis' many offerings each year.

Hyannis is also the starting point for the Cape Cod Railroad, a nostalgic steam train ride past the cranberry bogs, sand dunes and the Cape Cod Canal, with stops including Falmouth, Sandwich and West Barnstable. With its rail connections to Boston Rapid Transit and the Island ferries, the Cape Cod Railroad may help cut down traffic in the area.

Hyannis Port followed Falmouth as one of the first resort developments on the Cape. By the late 1800s, the wealthy were arriving in private railroad cars and steam yachts. This was an affluent summer playground long before Joseph Kennedy built the home that began the Kennedy Compound. The homes in the Compound are well shielded from the curious with shrubs and fences. A better reason to visit Hyannis Port is for the harbor view open to all from Sunset Hill.

Serene moments on Hyannis harbor **right** and **above far right** and one of the handsome old homes, Captain Cobb House **below right** that still grace the town that has become the busy shopping, entertainment and transportation hub of the Cape. Six million visitors pass through Hyannis every year.

When the late Ambassador Joseph P. Kennedy purchased his summer home in Hyannisport in 1926, he never dreamed that it would become part of one of the best-known residential complexes in the world. The Kennedy Compound, with the Ambassador's original home and the homes of John and Robert Kennedy and other family members, is now hidden behind fences and shrubs, but is retains its mystique and appeal for the public. Since it is best viewed today from the water, it has become a prime sight-seeing attraction on harbor cruises.

Paper Birch The white bark was once used by Indians to cover their canoes. The name derives from the quality of the bark, which is shed naturally in paper flakes.

Osterville, Cotuit and Centerville are other peaceful well-to-do residential villages within Barnstable, while Craigville, with one of the best beaches on the south shore, is a tourist town, along with parts of Yarmouth.

Yarmouth

Yarmouth is another town of many parts. The Indian Burial Ground in South Yarmouth marks a time when this area was heavily populated by Indians until war and disease took their toll. A stone marker here tells the tale: "On this slope lie buried the last native Indians of Yarmouth."

South Yarmouth later was a Quaker stronghold, and an 1809 meetinghouse remains, as does the ancient Judah Baker windmill. The shallow water at Smuggler's Beach in Bass River, which is actually part of South Yarmouth, proved an ideal site for the Colonists to smuggle in goods, evading British taxes. During Prohibition, rum runners found the beach equally useful.

Over on the north shore, Yarmouth Port is of particular interest for its exceptional Colonial architecture. Fifty sea captains once lived along the mile-long stretch of Route 6A in Yarmouth Port that was known as Captains' Row. One of their homes, the restored and treasure-filled Captain Bangs Hallet House, is now the home of the Historical Society of Old Yarmouth. Right next door are the Botanic Trails leading into two miles of forest, field and pond areas, a juxtaposition that typifies the Cape's blend of history and nature.

The trails remain thanks to a grant from a descendant of an early resident, Colonel John Thacher, whose 1664 home is also open to the public in Yarmouth Port. Another home of interest is the 1780 Winslow Crocker home with its secret gun room, now maintained by the Society for the Preservation of New England Antiquities.

The center of Yarmouth Port holds many other interesting sites. The "New Church" dates to the 1800s, and the Village Pump built

One of the finest homes
on Yarmouth Port's 'Captains' Row' is the
1740 Captain Bangs Hallet
House **above** , now the antique-filled
headquarters for the Historical
Society of Old Yarmouth.

Colonel John Thacher, son of one of Yarmouth's first settlers, helped populate the town by fathering 21 children. His handsome Colonial home **left**, built in 1664, is now open to the public.

in 1886 has supplied the town with water for many years.

![Dennis]

Dennis once again is typical of the split personality and confusing geography of Cape Cod towns. The north side has open meadows, marshes and the atmosphere of a quaint New England village. The south side is jammed with beach cottages and tourists.

There are four separate villages, all running into each other. South Dennis' main attraction for sightseers is the oldest working organ in the United States in its South Parish Congregational Church. West Dennis, which is actually south of South Dennis, has one of the best beaches on the south shore, meaning that it, too, is crowded, but it boasts Jericho House, a particularly fine example of an 1801 full Cape,

with a barn museum behind that has exhibits of the early saltmaking and cranberry industries on the Cape.

Dennis was prominent in both industries, thanks to two of its early residents. One, Henry Hall, is credited with developing the commercial growing of cranberries here in 1816. Captain Richard Sears, the man who began the saltmaking industry on the Cape, was also from Dennis, and his old home remains on North Street in what is now East Dennis.

The first Dennis was named for Reverend Josiah Dennis, pastor of the First Meeting House of Yarmouth, whose restored home also remains in town. Like its north shore neighbors, Yarmouth and Yarmouth Port, Dennis and East Dennis have many fine ship captains' homes, and many fine clipper ships were built right here at the Shiverick Shipyards in the mid-1800s.

The 19-mile Cape Cod Rail Trail, the best biking trail on the Cape, begins in Dennis and runs through woodland and cranberry bog to Brewster, Harwich and Orleans, ending at the National Seashore Salt Pond Visitor's Center in Eastham. The Fresh Pond Conservation area here is the perfect place to get away from it all.

Ruby-throated Hummingbird The only eastern species of hummingbird, this tiny creature is particularly attracted by red flowers.

53

The Jericho House in Dennis **right** is said to have acquired its name because before its restoration the walls were tumbling down. The 1801 Cape Cod home contains floor boards up to two feet wide.

Many sea captains worshipped at the 1835 South Parish Congregational Church **center**. A plaque inside lists 102 captains who lived in or near South Dennis, many of whom are buried in the cemetery just outside the church with markers reading simply 'lost at sea.' The church boasts the country's oldest working organ.

Dennis is also the home of the Cape Playhouse, another of the major dramatic showcases each summer.

The last part of the town is Dennisport, once filled with sailmakers and ship chandlers, now a typical Cape mix of rose-covered weathered Cape Cod cottages, lovely beaches and lots of tourist shops.

Harwich

Once again, there is more than one Harwich. In fact, there are seven, stretching across as a kind of buffer zone between the Mid- and Lower Cape. Some of the town has the charm of a painted scene—wild roses, Victorian homes and windmills. Wychmere Harbor is a particularly scenic spot and a favorite of photographers. Other parts of town feature go-carts and miniature golf, another typical Cape Cod mix.

Harwich has protected many of the cranberry bogs that are a major source of income locally, and bike trails weave for miles through the uplands above the bogs. A town conservation area at the head of the Herring River is ideal for canoeing.

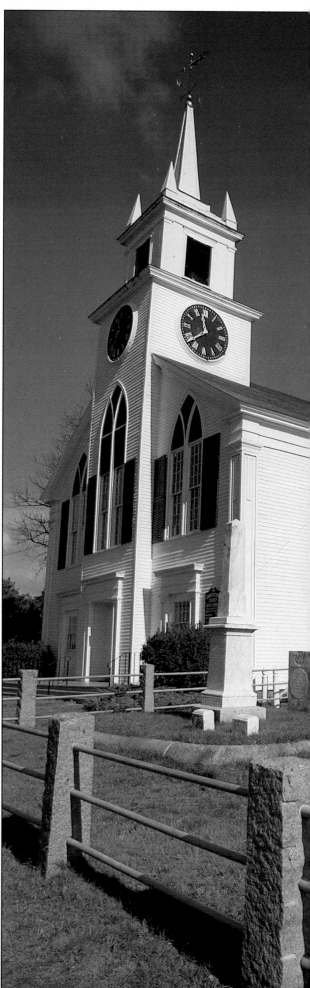

Cape Cod is the heart of America's cranberry harvest. Bogs can be seen throughout the area and ripening berries in the fall lend a deepening ruby-red blush to the landscape. Originally ripe berries were picked by long-toothed wooden scoops **above**. Today the work is done by machine or by the newer 'wet harvesting' method that loosens the berries by flooding so that they can be easily collected **middle** and **right**. The quality test for a cranberry has not changed with the years. The best berries are those that bounce.

East Dennis community church,
a particularly fine example of a colonial
church.

A view of Brewster's Old
Higgins windmill, a smock-type mill with a cap
of framing timbers curved
like the hull of a ship. It's a favorite subject
for Cape photographers
and artists.

A peaceful scene at Wychmere Harbor, Harwich **right** and another view of Brewster's Old Higgins windmill **center**.

Brewster

Brewster continues the north shore parade of fine captains' homes. Once part of Harwich, it was settled in 1656 but did not officially become the Town of Brewster until 1803. Georgian, Greek Revival and Victorian homes are evidence of the prosperous trade that went out from Brewster's harbor. The Elijah Cobb home on Lower Road is a Georgian mansion with a widow's walk that is a classic of its kind. Mill Pond, an idyllic spot marked by

Stony Brook Mill, a restored 1873 grist mill, is another setting that invites photographs.

Brewster is a favorite rainy day destination for its interesting museums. The Drummer Boy, a 35-acre site on the bay, has 21 ten-foot-high paintings of American Revolution scenes and a working eighteenth-century windmill. The Cape Cod Museum of Natural History offers live animals and marine exhibits, and the New England Fire and History Museum features early fire-fighting equipment and a diorama of the Chicago fire, along with replicas of a nineteenth-century blacksmith and apothecary shops on a recreated village common.

Sealand, with its sea lions and dolphin shows, is another popular local attraction.

Old Cape Cod can still be seen in picturesque settings such as Mill Pond in Brewster **left**, where the restored 1873 Stony Brook Mill stands on the site of the Cape's first grist mill, circa 1663.

THE LOWER CAPE

The beach-lovers' Cape begins here at the "elbow" along the shores of the Atlantic Ocean. This is the region where the National Seashore has preserved so much fragile beauty, and also a region rich in atmosphere from its romantic past. Each town has its attractions: Chatham for charm and water views, Orleans for its beach, old architecture and many shops and restaurants, Wellfleet for its galleries and great expanses of unspoiled landscape, Truro for its seclusion and wildness and Provincetown, "land's end" on the Cape, for the most fascinating history of all.

Chatham

In Chatham there seems to be water, water, everywhere—and no wonder. There are 67 miles of shore for 16 square miles of land. Historic homes here look out on Pleasant Bay and the Sound. At the end of Bridge Street, there are views of Chatham Light and the harbor, on the bluff a view of the Atlantic. Stage Harbor is the spot where Samuel Champlain landed on his ill-fated visit. Along Shore Road elegant old hotels and cottages share the view with summer mansions. Frequent fogs give it all the quality of a misty dream.

Offshore is Monomoy Island, a sandbar reaching ten miles out to sea. This barrier beach, which can be reached only by boat, is a National Wildlife refuge that is an important resting spot for migratory birds. Some 252 species have been spotted here. Morris Island, another nature-lovers' haven, is between the mainland and Monomoy.

As the furthest town on Route 28 on the south shore, Chatham has been spared the commercialism of her upper neighbors and remains a gracious village with fashionable shops and the scent of honeysuckle in the air. One of the special pleasures here is to walk down to the public observation deck at Aunt Lydia Cove to watch as the local fishing fleet brings in its catch of cod, haddock and flounder.

Chatham has preserved some of its history in the 1752 Old Atwood House on Stage Harbor Road, with everything from murals of New

In Chatham harbor **right**, hard-working fishermen are the inheritors of a long seafaring tradition, still bringing in some five million pounds of fish every year.

Chatham's Railroad Museum **opposite** offers memorabilia from early railroading days on the Cape, displayed in a nostalgic Victorian station house that was in service from 1887 to 1937.

On a bluff high over the Atlantic Ocean, Chatham Light **right** has guided seamen for over a century. Fine sea captains' homes bear witness to days when the town was a major fishing port.

One of Chatham's many handsome historic homes is the Atwood House **center**, circa 1752, now the home of the Chatham Historical Society and a repository for treasures from the town's past.

England life to a shell collection. The windmill in Chase Park dates back to 1797 and is a local landmark.

The drive along Route 28 along Pleasant Bay from Chatham to Orleans is the most scenic portion of this over-populated highway.

Orleans.

All roads lead to Orleans, the town where Route 6A and 28 and Route 6, the Mid-Cape Highway, converge.

The story goes that Orleans received its French name in honor of the Duke of Orleans after the French Revolution. Once part of Eastham, it was settled in 1693 and was a shipping, fishing and salt-producing center. Like Falmouth, Orleans defied British orders in the War of 1812. In Orleans, the bullying British were captured.

The comings and goings of the colorful boats in Chatham harbor **left** are an endless source of fascination for visitors.

Below Fishing floats form a bright montage in Orleans harbor.

Fine homes and churches may be found on any of the broad, shaded streets of Orleans **opposite**.

Spring in Nauset Marsh **above left** marks the arrival of winged creatures, wildflowers and a new coat of green for the marsh grasses as the National Seashore dons the colors of the new season. A nature trail from the Salt Pond Visitors Center in Eastham leads through the swamp and its tidal flats teeming with shore birds and sea life.

Visitors who come to savor the pensive beauty of sunset at Rock Harbor in Orleans **above right** often are unaware that this peaceful spot was the site of a naval battle during the War of 1812.

Below A Morgan horse stands ready on the village green to give visitors a tour around Falmouth.

Orleans also has the dubious distinction of being the only place in America to have been fired upon by the Germans in World War I. Having survived all enemies, it has grown into the shopping center of the Lower Cape. But while the center may bustle and has been invaded by fast-food outlets and discount stores, Orleans remains a town of great charm. The sections toward Rock Harbor and Cape Cod Bay, where early packet boats landed from Boston, is filled with gray-shingled cottages and white-picket fences. Fishing boats are still a constant presence in the pretty harbor.

The lanes of East Orleans are equally attractive, and Nauset Beach, the first major beach within the National Seashore, is as fine a stretch of dune-backed sand as can be found on any coast, wide open for walking as far as the eye can see and the feet can carry you.

The Cape's oldest remaining windmill installed in its own small park **below** the School House Museum with its famous whale's jaw entry **opposite** and the 1741 Swift-Daley House **above right** bear witness to Eastham's historic place as one of the four original settlements on Cape Cod.

Eastham

Eastham was one of the four original settlements on Cape Cod, and the place where a party of Mayflower Pilgrims met their first Indians, but you would hardly know it today. The Route 6 highway unfortunately runs right through the heart of town, obscuring its proud past. Only the Cape's oldest remaining windmill in the center of town, the Historical Society Museum and the Swift Daley House, a 1741 Cape Cod house, bear witness to the town's antiquity. The windmill is a special source of local pride and residents celebrate "Windmill Weekend" every autumn.

Currently Eastham is best known for its magnificent beaches and the National Seashore headquarters located here right off Route 6. The Seashore also encompasses Wellfleet, Truro, Provincetown and some parts of Orleans.

Wellfleet

With most of its land protected by the National Seashore, Wellfleet has not only exquisite beaches but also miles of wild and open moors thick with bayberry and blueberry shrubs. The Audubon Society wildlife sanctuary on the bay side offers 700 acres with trails through the moors and the marshes. Great Island, where whalers used to congregate, is now connected to the peninsula and can be explored via a trail.

Once a whaling and oystering center (some say the name came from "whale fleet," rather than from its English counterpart), Wellfleet has turned into the Cape's art gallery, with its historic main street filled with shops displaying work by Cape artists. A recent guide listed 18 galleries for art, crafts and sculptures and another five selling handicrafts or antiques.

Shops aside, the restrictions of the National Seashore have slowed tourist development so that Wellfleet remains a peaceful village of fine old homes. There are several distinctive churches on the main street, one of them with a town clock that strikes "ship's time," thought to be the only one of its kind. An old cemetery bears witness to the caprices of the sea among Wellfleet's early settlers, the Historical Society Museum has its own share of memories of early days, and Rider House nearby depicts life on the Cape of old, with a barn full of early farming and carpentry tools and an herb garden.

Overleaf Off-season visitors find a more tranquil Cape Cod and a real-life gallery of Currier and Ives scenes such as this portrait of Wellfleet dressed in white following a winter snowstorm.

Wellfleet's handsome and historic town center **near right** has bloomed anew as the home of dozens of galleries showing off the watercolors, oils, sculptures and crafts of talented Cape Cod artists.

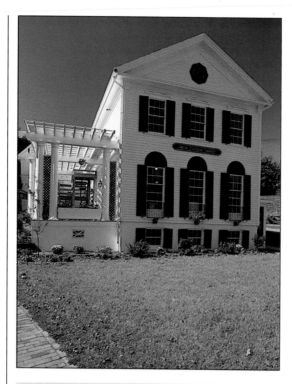

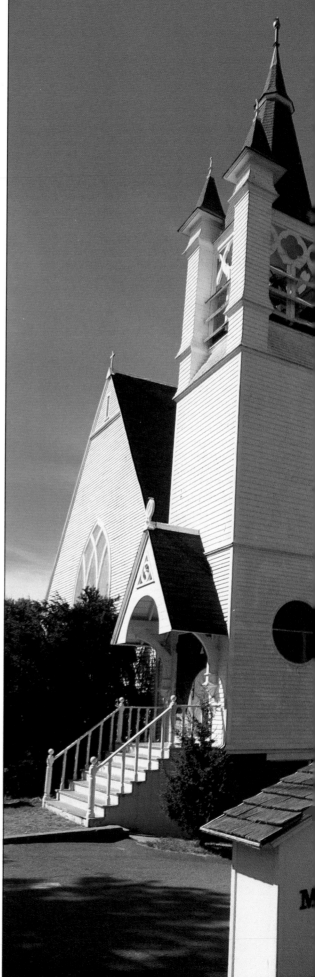

Truro

There is hardly a "town" to Truro. Beyond the highway, it is a world of moors, hills, valleys and rivers, its homes hidden amongst the trees. The beauty and solitude attract great numbers of psychiatrists who spend their annual August vacations in homes here.

On Corn Hill there is a tablet marking the spot where a party led by Myles Standish signalled the Mayflower of their safety after two days of exploring. The Pilgrim Heights area of the National Sea Shore marks the route of these early visitors near Pilgrim Lake, now a dramatic site rimmed by the dunes on its northeastern shore.

The Cape's first lighthouse was erected high on a bluff in Truro. It has been rebuilt twice, but the beams from Highland Lighthouse remain the strongest of all Cape Cod's guiding beacons for ships at sea.

From Truro, the last stop on the Cape and the continent is Provincetown.

Besides its artistic lures for browsers, Wellfleet offers many architectural treasures including fine churches and residences dating back to the eighteenth and early nineteenth centuries. Pictured here: The Methodist Church **center**, The Bradford Hotel **above** and an 1826 home **below**.

On a clear day, Provincetown's Pilgrim Monument **right** honoring the Mayflower pilgrims offers a view from its tower across the Cape to Plymouth Harbor where the Mayflower made its final landing.

A town for artists, fishermen, beach and beauty lovers, history buffs and escapists of all kinds, Provincetown **center** offers in its rich history and diversity something to please almost everyone.

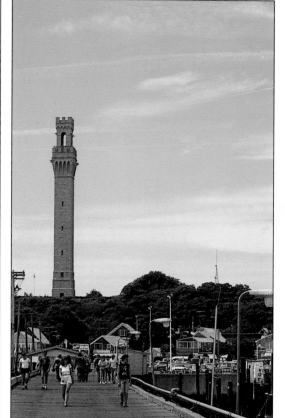

Provincetown

Harpooning a whale While the whaling industry is no more, you can still take whale-watching expeditions from Provincetown.

Indians, explorers, Pilgrims, fishermen, whalers, artists, writers, beach-lovers, pleasure-seekers, escapists—all have found their way to Provincetown. The town at the extreme tip of Cape Cod has so much history and has inspired so many legends that it becomes difficult to separate the facts from the fictions.

Some say that Thorvald, Leif Erickson's brother, came ashore here to repair the keel of his boat during the Viking era in 1004 A.D. and named the place "Cape of the Keel." Some say that the tradition of Monday as washday began when the Pilgrims came ashore in Provincetown on a Monday in 1620 to tidy up after their long voyage.

What is known for sure and verified by monuments all over town is that the Pilgrims made their first stop here and drew up the Mayflower Compact offshore, affirming their belief in law and self-government in a document said to be the root of democractic government in America.

The spot where they first set foot in the New World at the west end of what is now Commercial Street is marked by a bronze plaque set in a boulder, and a bas-relief on Bradford Street behind the Town Hall depicts the signing of the Mayflower Compact, the "first American Act in our History." The Pilgrim Monument commemorating the landing, the tallest granite structure in the nation, was dedicated in 1910. The 255-foot tower dominates the town and has become a landmark for visitors, noted for the view from the top across the Cape to Plymouth.

A FISHERMEN'S TOWN

During the 1600 and 1700s, Provincetown was settled by men pursuing mackerel and cod. The early comers built their simple Cape Cod homes close to the bay near the water with the beach as their main highway and side streets running inland. In the early years, shore fishing and beach whaling were the main activities, but by 1760 deep-water fishing and whal-

A figurehead that once stood proudly on the bow of a ship now looks out to sea from one of the many weathered fishermen's cottages that line the narrow lanes of Provincetown.

ing were coming of age, and a dozen whalers and a cod-fishing fleet had headquarters in Provincetown.

By the time of the American Revolution, Provincetown had about 20 houses and 200 residents, and there were several encounters here between Colonial militia and the forces of the British who controlled the harbor. The British frigate *Somerset*, known for her bombardment of Bunker Hill, used Provincetown Harbor as a home port for attacking raids on Continental and French ships. She went aground east of Race Point and was wrecked in 1778. Her remains still lie beneath the sand, where shifting currents occasionally briefly uncover the remains.

After the war, the town grew into one of the greatest and busiest seaports in the country, its Grand Banks fishing fleets and whaling expeditions coexisting on the bustling waterfront. In the middle of the nineteenth century, the development of trap fishing, particularly the nets used to scoop up huge numbers of mackerel, spurred things even further. By 1851, 56 wharves jutted into the bay, and the waterfront was lined with buildings for smoking, canning and curing fish. Salt was supplied by 70 saltworks, many powered by windmills

along the waterfront. Fishermen from Portugal and from Nova Scotia had joined the Yankees, and their descendants still influence the flavor of the town. The great wealth brought from the sea was responsible for many of the fine Victorian, Second Empire, Gothic and Greek Revival homes that are now inns or restaurants in town.

Though whaling declined in the late 1800s, the whales remain offshore and nowadays whale-watching expeditions are a favorite Provincetown activity. The fishing industry continues to prosper also and still accounts for some 11 million pounds of cod, mackerel, flounder and other fish brought into the same historic pier each year that had served earlier generations, now called MacMillan Wharf. The fishing fleet goes out early each morning and returns in the late afternoon, a picturesque sight that has hardly changed in 100 years.

The Portuguese custom of the Blessing of the Fleet also continues on the last Sunday each June, beginning with a Solemn High Mass and followed by a colorful procession from the church to the wharf by the fishermen and townspeople carrying a statue of Saint Peter, patron of fishermen. The entire fleet then sails in gaily decorated boats past the wharf.

AN ARTISTS' TOWN

If the fishermen gave Provincetown its first identity, it was the artists and writers who added a new dimension to the town. Drawn by the brilliant light and wealth of subjects, Charles W. Hawthorne started it all with his Cape Cod School of Painting in 1899. The Provincetown Art Association, established in 1914, has a current membership list that is a *Who's Who* of the American art world and an outstanding permanent collection of 500 works, as well as exhibits by emerging artists. There are two other major galleries and any number of minor ones. Among the luminaries who have painted here are Max Bohm, Edwin Dickinson, Hans Hofmann, Edward Hopper and Robert Motherwell, who has a home at the end of Commercial Street.

Writers followed the artists. One of the first was a passing visitor, Henry David Thoreau, who came in 1849 and wrote about the "Great Beach" that remains a prominent feature of the town. In 1916 John Reed and Louise Bryant came to what has been called "this refuge for

Overleaf Provincetown's harbor was world-renowned for its fishing fleet and whalers. The fleet can still be seen setting out each morning for a catch that nets a prodigious eleven million pounds of cod, mackerel, flounder and other bounty from the sea.

Right Fishermen's cottages and fine summer homes mingle happily in Provincetown, a town that delights artist, angler and beach-lover alike with its mix of moods and attractions.

The busy and bountiful fishing fleet that goes out daily from Provincetown **below** leaves and lands at the same historic docks that served many of their ancestors more than a century ago.

New York's avant garde" and brought with them their friend, a young playwright named Eugene O'Neill. The play that launched O'Neill's career, *Bound East for Cardiff*, was performed by the Provincetown Players at the wharf that summer.

O'Neill was just one of the writers and poets who discovered Provincetown in this century. John Dos Passos, Max Eastman, Sinclair Lewis, Norman Mailer, Tennessee Williams and poet Stanley Kunitz, another current Commercial Street resident, are among them.

Many performers developed their talents in Provincetown also. The long list includes Wally Cox, Marlon Brando, Eartha Kitt, Al Pacino, Bobby Short and the late Billie Holliday.

ROOM FOR ALL

Artists and writers and the fishing population continue to contribute to the colorful mix of people who mingle on Commercial Street these days, and though the original historic Playhouse was a victim of a 1976 fire, the Provincetown Players continue to attract talented young people. The town's beauty, easygoing air and freedom of spirit has, in fact, attracted many kinds of people over the years who mingle here happily—and many tourists who come to see them all. The local Chamber of Commerce may have described the current street scene best in their own brochure, which promises "at least two of everything. Tall. Short. Fat. Slim. Dressy. Simple. Gay. Straight. Families. Singles. Old. Young."

A stroll through town armed with the walking tour guide put out by the local Historical Society shows all of this mixture—the old homes that have been lovingly kept up by their owners over the generations, the gardens alive with old-fashioned blooms, the fishing boats, the monuments, the passing people parade on Commercial Street and the myriad restaurants and shops that accommodate the many who come to experience all that Provincetown has to offer.

For most, what it offers beyond all else is the magnificent beaches and dunes that shift with the winds and erode with the tides but were here in their spectacular beauty long before the Pilgrims came. With care, they may remain for centuries to come.

Shifting sands and seascapes **above** and **center** at 'land's end' — the spectacular shores of Provincetown at the furthest tip of Cape Cod.

NATURE'S BOUNTY

When the first settlers arrived in Provincetown, they found a land of good soil and plentiful timber. But here and throughout the Cape, they overestimated and overused these riches. By the mid-1800s, development had depleted vast areas of forest and woodlands. Shipbuilding and the saltworks which required trees as fuel to evaporate salt from the sea water were responsible for the wanton cutting of trees. Overplanting without replenishing had also diminished the richness of the soil.

The land around Eastham and Wellfleet that Thoreau described in the 1850s as "a desert ... a pure sand plateau without a particle of vegetation" was not nature's work but the result of exploitation by early inhabitants. The overworking of sandy soil that was poor in the first place has meant that farming has all but disappeared as an occupation.

However, nature repaired much of man's damage with new growth. Pitch pine, scrub oak and beech replaced the lost trees, and much of the natural beauty of other areas has been retained through the establishment of the Cape Cod National Seashore and other nature preserves. Despite the continued growth of tourism, today's Cape remains a paradise for nature lovers with 357 species of birds, untold numbers of fish in its waters and flora and fauna of all kinds waiting to be discovered.

The seasons are marked on the Cape in a rainbow of colors from its plants, flowering shrubs and trees. In spring, the bountiful beach plum bursts into a border of low-growing white blooms near the shore and along roadsides everywhere, and Cape Cod houses are enveloped in the pinks and purples of azalea, dogwood, rhododendron, laurels and lilacs that grow in their yards and canopy their roofs.

Around the ponds, woody shrubs like highbush blueberry, sweet pepper bush, button bush and sheep laurel thrive, and in summer water lilies cover the surface of the ponds, their pads providing resting spots for frogs and damsel flies and hiding places for fish and turtles.

The wild roses of summer are augmented by the lush annual gardens whose tending seems to be a natural talent of Cape Cod residents. In towns like Orleans, even the souvenir shops are brightened by pots of geraniums and rows of marigolds and zinnias in brilliant colors.

In fall, the season many natives love best, the cranberry bogs turn to the color of wine, the beach plums and wild cherries ripen to ruby red, the leaves on the bearberry vines turn to bronze and the seaside goldenrod bursts into bloom, a show that opens somewhat ironically just about the time the summer season is coming to a close.

When winter quiet blankets the Cape, still another face emerges. It is when the visitors leave that the quiet old seafaring towns can catch their collective breaths and regain their identities, free from the pressures of summer rush.

Except for a rare solitary sturdy survivor, the fertile forests of tall trees are gone, but many kinds of trees of the beach landscape remain on the Cape, beginning right beyond the dunes. Twisted pitch pines and scrub oaks make a miniature forest to shelter shade-loving plants and dozens of variety of birds. The trees fight an endless battle with the wind-blown sand that threatens to envelop them.

The scrub oaks never grow more than ten feet high, but away from salt spray, the pines can reach a height of 50 feet. On the Upper Cape, forests of tall pines and holly can be seen, protected in many nature preserves. The marshlands on the Cape produce their own varieties of trees such as willows, alders, red maples and black gums.

The variety of environments means that bird watchers also find Cape Cod a land of abundant riches, with saltwater and freshwater marshes, bogs, forest, ponds and shore areas all attracting residents. Terns, black skimmers, marsh hawks, Canada geese, black-crowned night herons, clape rails, black ducks, song sparrows, bobwhites and barn swallows are just a few of the hundreds of species that have been spotted on the wing and in the many preserves around the Cape and the Islands. The Massachusetts Audubon Society has headquarters in Wellfleet, where a large bayside sanctuary offers blinds for bird watching and photography.

The gulls and sandpipers at the shore are familiar to all beach lovers and are the subjects of countless Cape Cod souvenir snapshots.

The shores of the Cape also hold a bounty of treasures for beachcombers. The bay and

Black Skimmer This striking black-and-white bird has a bright red beak and is often to be seen skimming along the surface of the water.

Opposite 'Sconset's unique charm brought many notable vacationers in the late 1800s, including a colony of well-known actors. The serentiy that attracted them remains a lure to visitors today.

Even the humblest shingled Cape Cod cottage is brightened by blooms most of the year from bounteous gardens like these in Provincetown **right** and **center below** that are matched in every Cape town and village.

sound waters yield the most perfect shells: whelks, arks, pandoras, crabs, quahogs, razor clams, moon and mud snails, angel wings, oysters, scallops, mussels, starfish, periwinkles, purple snails, sand dollars and sea urchins, all to be had by those patient collectors who wait for their prizes to be handed out by the sea.

Abundant sea life in Cape waters sustained the early settlers. It has been a means of livelihood for generations of Cape fishermen and pleased the palates of countless numbers of visitors. There is an unusual profusion of marine life due to the meeting of two currents in offshore waters—the Labrador current flowing down the New England Coast with chilled Arctic temperatures, and the Gulf Stream, which flows up from the south, swinging east to cross the Atlantic near Nantucket, moderating the winter climate for the Cape and the Islands.

Thus cold-water creatures like lobsters can exist off-shore, along with seals, dolphins, porpoises and whales. And cod, mackerel, herring, bluefish, swordfish, tuna and striped bass also thrive in Cape waters, while shrimp, crabs and scallops are plentiful in the shallow waters close to shore.

Despite the development that is changing some areas of Cape Cod and its Islands, much of this natural bounty and beauty remains, particularly in the preserves. Many are the gifts of early residents who loved the Cape and its landscape. This foresight and generosity has saved the wonders of a fragile ecology for us today and for our children tomorrow. The National Seashore is just one of the retreats where nature's gifts to the Cape can still be seen.

Ashumet, Lowell and Wakeby Holly Reservations

The Massachusetts Audubon Society was entrusted with the 45-acre collection of holly species collected from throughout the Cape and the Islands by the late Wilfred Wheeler. Nature trails in the East Falmouth Ashumet Reservation lead past dozens of varieties of Oriental and European hollies and other native plants, as well as a world of ponds, wild-flowers and flowering shrubs and trees that change their displays with the seasons. Pink lady's slipper, magnolias and dogwoods are part of the show. Catbirds are attracted to the thick trees and shrubbery near the water, and their mewing calls keep walkers company, along with the chattel of kingfishers.

The Lowell Holly Reservation near Sandwich is a 130-acre peninsula that divides Wakeby and Mashpee Ponds, two of the Cape's largest freshwater ponds. Abbott Lawrence Lowell, president of Harvard University from 1909 to 1933, presented the property to the Trustees of Reservations in 1943, preserving its many varieties of pines and hollies and a pristine woodland that abounds with the calls of towhees, catbirds, flickers and waterfowl who live on the ponds. Azaleas, mountain laurel and rhododendrons burst forth in a showy display every spring. The ferns are a constant show, nature's way of adorning her damp and shady areas.

There are 145 acres of woodland filled with native holly trees 50 feet high and up to 150 years old, as well as stands of smooth-barked

Top center Seals can frequently be sighted off the coast of Cape Cod, along with dolphins, porpoises and whales. Cruises to spot the playful sea life in Cape waters are increasingly popular.

Overleaf Endlessly mesmerizing patterns of sand and sea await visitors to the Cape Cod National Seashore, where more than 50 miles of beaches are preserved and protected in their natural state.

Belted Kingfisher This grey-crested bird hovers erratically over streams and lakes and plunges headfirst into the water to catch fish. **81**

Sassafras The aromatic twigs, bark and roots of this genus are used to produce fragrant oil and tea. Native to the east, it grows up to 75ft.

beeches and towering pines in the Wakeby Holly Sanctuary and Recreation Area that was acquired by the Sandwich Conservation Commission in 1975. Wakeby Pond is prime territory for freshwater fishermen, and swimming and boating as well as fishing are allowed within the recreation area.

The Old Briar Patch

Peter Rabbit wanders the trail of the Old Briar Patch in the tales told by noted children's writer Thorton Burgess, a Sandwich native. The 57-acre woodland dedicated to Mr. Burgess in 1974 is the area where his love of nature and the scenes of his stories originated. It remains an area full of prickly hiding places for cottontail rabbits, and the nature trails meander through woods of giant pine and swamplands hardly touched by time. A clearing in the pines near Discovery Hill is a secluded spot for contemplating the natural setting that inspired Mr. Burgess.

John Wing Trail

Brewster's earliest settlers found the marsh hay on Wing's Island important as feed for their cattle and mulch for their lands. The town of Brewster has proteced this 33-acre upland and its 90 acres of beach and salt marsh for all to enjoy today as a retreat and recreational area. A walk along twisted trails between the pitch pines and bearberry bushes provides a number of vantage points for exceptional views, as well as the chance to observe life along the salt marsh and the sassafras grove near its edge. The roots and bark of the sassafras were used in the old days to make tea that was a popular tonic for ailing

pioneers. More forest and marshland nature trails are to be found at Brewster's Cape Cod Museum of Natural History.

Sandy Neck

The six miles of dunes at Sandy Neck off Cape Cod Bay in Barnstable are said to date back 4,000 years, and the equally awesome 3,000-acre Great Marshes they shelter are almost as old. The ever-changing shapes of the dunes can reach mini-mountain proportions, and the marshes protect a prodigious variety of sea and land birds and marine life. Swimmers, sunbathers, beachcombers, hikers and fishermen can all enjoy this exceptional setting.

Harding Beach Seaside Trail

Views of ocean surf, barren dunes, beach plums, salt marsh and the Oyster River await walkers on the Seaside Trail maintained by the Chatham Conservation Foundation. Birds abound here, including the unusual horned lark, which breeds in the sparsely vegetated areas of some of the more barren dunes.

The National Seashore

Stripped of its protective forests, its farmlands and meadows depleted by overuse, the lower portion of Cape Cod had been left to contend not only with the elements but also with ever-

Nauset Light **left**, separated by a cliff from the National Seashore beach below, is a red and white sentinel whose sweeping beam lights a particularly dangerous section of the North Atlantic.

85

Officially, the National Seashore covers 27,000 acres of land
and more than 50 miles of beach. Because it includes many areas that had
already become residential before 1961 and because it takes
jurisdiction for much of their own land away from the towns of Eastham,
Wellfleet and Truro, the Seashore is somewhat controversial,
but no one can argue with the result, which is one of the world's most fabulous
and fascinating seashore environments. The Seashore has not
only encompassed beaches, but also the wetlands, swamps, marshes and
dunes that surround them, preserving the entire fragile ecological
system for the edification and enjoyment of visitors.

Left The Pavilion at the Marconi Wireless State Site, part of the Cape Cod National Seashore at Wellfleet, marks the spot where the first wireless communication between Europe and America took place in 1903. The original towers have disappeared with the restless tides.

increasing numbers of tourists who had the potential to drown it in motels and gift shops. In 1961, concerned conservationists convinced Congress to act to save this irreplaceable treasure, and the Cape Cod National Seashore was created.

The area also provides recreation and restorative beauty for swimmers, surfers, hikers, bikers and horseback riders as well as anyone who simply wants to sit on a solitary beach and contemplate the hypnotic rhythms of the sea. The well-tended trails are designed to show the variety of the terrain as well as the ever-changing effects of wind and water on the shore.

Nowhere is the power of erosion more clearly seen than at the Marconi Wireless State site at Wellfleet, where the Cape is only a mile wide. Much of the cliff has disappeared, along with the towers Guglielmo Marconi built there at the site of the first wireless communication between Europe and America in 1903. Each is a victim of the relentless tides that wash away an average of three feet of coastline every year.

The Marconi site leads into the Atlantic White Cedar Swamp Trail, where lush green vegetation surrounds walkers as they thread their way through the swamp on elevated boardwalks. There are many other trails taking in the salt ponds, forests and dunes. On the Nauset Swamp Path or any path, you are likely to be surprised with views of glimmering ponds or sweeping ocean vistas through a clearing.

There are four main areas of the Seashore. Nauset, located in Eastham, includes the main visitors' center, two beaches and a bike trail. The Marconi Site in South Wellfleet has its own beach and nature trails, including the White Cedar Swamp Trail. Pilgrim Heights in North Truro, another place to find beach and trails, also features a display of Indian artifacts. Most beautiful of all, and with the most spectacular of the dunes, is the Provincelands area approaching Provincetown. There are two more beaches here, trails through the dunes and an ocean view from the deck of the Information Center that is unforgettable, particularly at sunset.

The remoteness of this "land's end" outpost has special appeal. Many visitors choose to escape the world even further by visiting Martha's Vineyard and Nantucket, the islands at sea reached by ferryboat from the south coast of the Cape.

PART II

THE ISLANDS

INTRODUCTION

*R*obert Browning wrote of "some unsuspected isle in far-off seas ..."

There is something about an island, a sense of escape and romance, that appeals to almost everyone. Two of America's most extraordinary islands lie off the coast of Cape Cod, and their appeal seems to grow in direct proportion to the build-up and hurly-burly that needs escaping on the mainland.

Nantucket and Martha's Vineyard are sister islands, but they are far from twins in size, appearance or outlook.

Nantucket is relatively small and isolated, 30 miles out to sea and two-and-a-half hours by boat from the mainland. Nantucket town, the only real town on the island, still bears some of the influence of the Quakers who made up much of its early population, as well as its world pre-eminence as a whaling port. The town is perhaps the most perfect remaining Colonial enclave in America, one whose cobblestones, cottages and mansions have been preserved by an act of fate, yet a living, vital community whose historic backdrop enhances rather than encumbers summer visits.

The out-island is low and wild, a rugged land of heather on the moors, of ponds and bogs, a landscape rimmed by pounding ocean on one side, placid bay on the other and flawless beaches all around—indeed, an isle in far-off seas.

In contrast, Martha's Vineyard, only seven miles and 45 minutes from shore, is the biggest of all New England's vacation islands, more than twice the size of Nantucket. Though it shares a long maritime heritage, it was also a land of farms and pastures and later a Victorian seaside resort famous for its revival meetings. The island seems soft and green compared to Nantucket, with an interior of trees and fields and stone walls that might be at home in the Connecticut countryside. It is country retreat and beach resort in one, with its nature preserves, dramatic cliffs, prize sailing waters and a mix of architecture and moods as a bonus.

Instead of one town, there are three main centers on the Vineyard and three small ones. Except for the ubiquitous beauty, you can't categorize the towns or the island—which may be precisely why so many people love it. There is something for everyone.

Those who favor each island are not usually the same people, and each set of devotees tends to be passionate about their feelings. Vineyard people sniff about "cutesy cobblestones and scrubby landscapes" while Nantucket people snidely wonder why you need travel so far to find grass and green trees that grow at home. Both islands share the blessing of bountiful beaches and the problem of too much popularity which threatens the very serenity that makes them appealing.

Each holds its own rewards—and they are plentiful.

Opposite The windswept clay cliffs at Gay Head bear in their fossil imprints and kaleidoscope of colors a record of the evolution of the island and the visits of **90** glaciers, during the Ice Age.

MARTHA'S VINEYARD

Martha's Vineyard is an island of opposites, a place with the pastoral beauty of the English countryside and the pleasures of the sea. The beaches are unexcelled. The history is a mix of whaling lore and religious zeal, the population a blend of descendants of Indians and seamen and preachers and, in recent years, resident celebrities in the summer. There are all kinds of towns and all kinds of terrain to be explored.

Early History

The first men probably came to Martha's Vineyard even before it was an island, before the melting glaciers in the north raised the sea level separating it from the mainland. Indian camps that archaeologists date to about 2270 BC are still being found.

The Indians call it Noe-pe, "island in the streams." In 1524, Verrazzano sailed past, named the island Louisa and literally put it on his map. But the same Bartholomew Gosnold who named Cape Cod had his say here, too, in 1602, naming the island for the wild grapes that abounded and for one of his young daughters.

Many other explorers followed—Samuel Champlain, Adrian Block, Thomas Hunt, Thomas Dermer—all extolling the abundant fish and bird life, wild fruits and good timber they found here. Even the Indians seemed exemplary, described by one writer as "exceeding courteous, gentle of disposition and well condition, exceeding all others that we have seen ..."

In 1642, as all of New England was being claimed and divided, Thomas Mayhew, a businessman from Watertown, Massachusetts, bought the Vineyard, Nantucket and the Elizabeth Islands for the bargain price of £40. The first settlement at Great Harbor, now known as Edgartown, was led by Mayhew's son, Thomas, Jr.

The newcomers found a large and stable native population living in permanent villages. The Sachemship of Aquinnah comprised the present Gay Head; Tisbury was Takemmy, Nunpaug was Edgartown, and Chappaquiddick retains the name of the tribe that first lived there. The name, according to interpreters, appropriately means "an island place" or "a small separate island." All were part of the Wampanoag nation that followed the Great Sachem Massasoit on the mainland.

The Indians lived well, hunting, fishing and farming. They grew corn, beans and squash, fished and visited the mainland in their dugout canoes and used native wood and clay to fashion pottery and utensils.

As the ordained pastor of his flock, young Mayhew, like his father, was scrupulously fair with the natives, ruling that no land be taken without consent and fair payment. Because of the Mayhews, the island was spared the bloodshed that marked so many new settlements.

Local records report that here was where the first Indian was converted to one God, a native named Hiacoomes. In return for Mayhew's teaching him his faith and the English language, the Indian taught the pastor the native language. Hiacoomes helped Mayhew to spread the gospel, and within a few years a congregation of "Praying Indians" was established at what is still known as Christiantown, with Hiacoomes as pastor. Eventually, there was a whole staff of Indian preachers and schoolmasters. The population of natives who adopted Christianity reached 1,600.

Mayhew, unfortunately, was lost at sea on a voyage to England. The "Place by the Wayside" near the present airport is the spot where he said his last good-bye to the island Indians.

The early days on the island were a time of plenty as well as peace. The settlers cleared the land and built miles of stone walls, many of which remain today. Crops were bountiful and fish was plentiful in the surrounding waters. The Indians also taught the settlers how to take offshore whales on the beach to be dried for oil. Flocks of sheep and cows provided wool and leather for clothing and butter and cheese that could be exported, providing the income to purchase such luxuries as spices, sugar, coffee, tea and rum. For the necessities of living, the island was self-sufficient.

But as newcomers joined the original settlers, there were changes. Baptist and

Opposite Bicycles are a favorite means of exploring on Martha's Vineyard, with many bike paths providing a leisurely look at the island's surprising diversity of scenery, sea and landscapes.

The fine captains' homes that are to be seen in Edgartown are a reminder of the prosperous whaling industry that once existed here.

Methodist ministers challenged the established churches. The native population declined as diseases brought by the white men began to take their toll. And passing ships brought word of growing discord as the Colonists grew increasingly displeased with the rules and regulations laid down by the Crown.

The American Revolution brought hardship to the island. Vineyard residents took part in the struggle. One of the first naval engagements of the war took place in April 1775 when Nathan Smith of Tisbury mounted three small cannons on a whaleboat and sailed across Vineyard Sound to attack and capture the British schooner *Volante*.

The little island was vulnerable, however, and when the British sailed a fleet of 40 ships into Vineyard Haven, the colonists were no match. Their ships were burned and more than 10,000 sheep and 300 head of cattle were removed by the raiders, an economic blow that affected island life for many years afterwards.

Resurgence of Whaling

Before the war, Vineyard whalers had sailed their large ships from the Grand Banks to the Western islands, but the war disrupted the industry so badly that many families moved away to seek a new livelihood. It took time before whaling operations recovered, but the best whaling days were yet to come, and in the early 1820s, the glory years had arrived. While it did not equal Nantucket, Edgartown was important as a whaling center, and it was during this period that many of the captains built the fine homes that can still be seen here. According to one island history, "by 1825 the name of Edgartown was known around the globe as a whaling port and birthplace of doughty mariners."

As ships grew larger and voyages longer, adventurous captains sailing around the Horn to Pacific whaling grounds were gone for three or four years at a time. Often they took to bringing their wives and families with them,

A simple monument marks the 'Place by the Wayside', the spot where Thomas Mayhew, Jr., founder of the first settlement on Martha's Vineyard, said his last good-bye to the Indians he had befriended and converted to Christianity. Stones placed by the Indians in his memory were eventually cemented together as the memorial that now bears a bronze marker **left**. Single stones still serve as markers in the Indian Burying Ground nearby **center**.

resulting in many young babies returning to the Vineyard bearing exotic Oriental names. The returning ships also brought valuable cargoes of oil and whalebone as well as Chinese porcelain, carved ivory, camphor chests and other rare Oriental objects. Many of them are still treasured possessions in Island homes today.

The combination of the Civil War and the discovery of petroleum ended the whaling era, but Martha's Vineyard found a new industry in an unexpected way.

"God-Sent" Visitors

There were early visitors who were a sign of what was to come. Nathaniel Hawthorne spent most of the summer of 1835 on Martha's Vineyard and wrote about the island. Daniel Webster came in 1849, and in 1858 boats from the New York Yacht Club sailed in for the first of what was to become a regular cruise.

Center Sandpipers bring life to the scenic shores of Martha's Vineyard.

But the real tourist boom was inspired by prayer. In 1835, the Edgartown Methodists held a camp meeting in an oak grove high on the bluffs at the northern end of town. The worshippers and their preachers lived in improvised tents; the speakers' platform was made of driftwood. It was one of hundreds of such meetings being conducted in outdoor settings, but this one was particularly successful.

The camp meeting became an annual affair and began to grow. By 1859, the Martha's Vineyard Camp Meeting had become the largest in the world, with more than 12,000 attending. Those who came discovered that the sea air and surroundings were as inspiring as the meetings, and soon the island was booming as a summer resort.

The first development began in 1866, just as summer vacationing began to grow in popularity in America. Cottage City, as Oak Bluffs was first called, remained the center of island life for many years, its hotels and rooming houses providing accommodation for visitors who came to enjoy the beach, to dance at the Tivoli Ballroom and listen to the concerts from the bandstands. An excursion boat took them on all-day trips to see the cliffs at Gay Head, where the Indians met them in an oxcart. For a while, there was a railroad from Oak Bluffs to Katama along what is now the State Beach.

The Baptists joined the march to Martha's Vineyard and began holding summer sessions in Vineyard Highlands. The Martha's Vineyard Summer Institute planned educational meetings on the island, said to be the first summer school in the country. The Massachusetts Division of the League of American Wheelmen came to the island to meet, delighted with the many rural lanes for cycling. In more elegant Edgartown, the Harbor View Inn became a favorite for upper-class families.

In 1874, President Ulysses S. Grant proved that "everybody was doing it," visiting Martha's Vineyard to the tune of flags, bands and fireworks. The President was given a place of honor on the platform when he attended the Camp Meeting "Big Sunday" service in Oak Grove, the annual climax of the season.

Following the lead of Hawthorne and Webster, writers and other noted celebrities began to make their way to the Vineyard. W. Somerset Maugham and Yale President Whitney Griswold were among them. The line-up conti-

nues today: Katherine Graham of the *Washington Post*, James Reston of the *New York Times* (who also owns the *Vineyard Gazette*), humorist Art Buchwald, novelist William Styron, singer Carly Simon and opera star Beverly Sills. Jacqueline Kennedy Onassis recently joined the list, purchasing an estate in Gay Head.

The homes of these notables are private, carefully screened from public view. This is not an island for gawking at celebrities; there is too much else to do and see. There are six towns on Martha's Vineyard, each with its own special flavor.

Vineyard Haven

Most visitors get their first look at Martha's Vineyard aboard the ferries that make their way into the harbor of Vineyard Haven

between the two points of land known as East Chop and West Chop, each with its own landmark lighthouse. When clipper ships plied the seas, the harbor, then known as Holmes Hole, was a convenient anchorage for boats traveling along the coast through Vineyard Sound. Hundreds of such vessels might have been found where pleasure boats and ferries now anchor. Local "bumboats" prospered, carrying men and supplies between ship and shore.

The restored Seaman's Bethel, now a chapel and museum, was built as a sleeping place, social center and house of worship for sailors far from home. Among the sailing memorabilia and scrimshaw inside, there is a Mayhew family tree on the wall tracing the descendants of the island founders.

The little park overlooking the water is named for William Barry Owen, who made his fortune pioneering the gramophone as head of the Victor Talking Machine Company. The little town beach, named for one of Vineyard Haven's whaling captains, provides another place to watch the comings and goings in the harbor.

Across the street, an 1828 schoolhouse has been preserved by the Daughters of the Amer-

ican Revolution and turned into the Liberty Pole Museum, commemorating the daring of three village girls who blew up the town liberty pole with gunpowder in 1776 rather than allow the British to take it as a spar for their warships. The museum holds many pieces telling the story of the island's past.

The Congregationalists used the schoolhouse for their services until 1828, then built their own neoclassical building in 1844 on Spring Street. It was later a Unitarian Church, then the town hall and is now known as Association Hall, home of municipal offices and the town theater, named for actress Catherine Cornell who spent many years on the island.

Five miles from Vineyard Haven on the North Shore is Christiantown, the square mile set aside as a township for the new converts known as the "Praying Indians." At the end of Christiantown Road, almost hidden in the trees, is the chapel where they worshipped. It is named for Reverend Thomas Mayhew Jr., who was responsible for the conversion of the Indians. There is also a pulpit rock where the first services were held.

Congregation members were buried in the Indian Burial Ground here, their graves marked with fieldstones. The Martha's Vineyard Garden Club has marked the spot with a wildflower garden.

If Christiantown marks the island's past, Windfarm Museum on the road from Vineyard Haven to Edgartown is the future. A solar-heated, wind-powered home and organic garden show how latter-day pioneers are learning to make the most of nature's beauty.

Edgartown

Though the harbor is filled with yachts these days instead of whalers, the annual Edgartown Regatta is one of the premier yacht races on the coast. The shaded streets of Edgartown retain the look of a nineteenth-century seaport. It was the Vineyard's first white settlement and has remained the county seat since 1642. As the center of the whaling industry, it

The home of Dr. Daniel
Fisher **opposite** and **above** reflects wealth
that came from whaling
as well as healing. The richest man in early
Edgartown, he owned a
whale-oil refinery that was the nation's largest
maker of spermaceti candles
and also the supplier of whale oil to all of
America's lighthouses. He
also founded the island's first bank.

Whaling days left their unmistakable imprint on Edgartown **right**, where fine sea captains' mansions may be found at every turn. The many imposing white Greek Revival homes of the golden era of the whalers bear the dark shutters, fanlights and 'widow's walks' typical of the period

was the home of the sea captains and merchants who made their fortunes at sea, and their homes remain to remind of the glory days of the whaling ships.

A walk along its lanes is a tour past Greek Revival homes of that whaling heyday, still replete with their dark shutters, fanlights and the "widow's walks" where worried wives watched for their husbands' return from sea. Rose-covered picket fences add charm to the scene.

Main Street with its harbor and waterfront still bears the imprint of whaling days, though nowadays there are as many galleries and shops as nautical emporiums. Water Street, which parallels the harbor, has mansions and a huge pagoda tree brought from China as a seedling in the early days of the last century. One of the houses on South Water Street belonged to Captain Valentine Pease, master of the ship on which Herman Melville, author of *Moby Dick*, made his only whaling voyage.

Many of the structures predate the whaling era. Three of the most notable now serve as museums and the office of the *Vineyard Gazette*. The Federated Church, built in 1828,

The Old Burying Ground of the Federated Church **left** tells the tale of many of the island's early settlers.

Beach dwellings on Martha's Vineyard **center** come in many shapes and forms. With hues and mood shifting with the time and the tide, the island's beaches are a constant glory.

still has its old box pews with narrow seats entered through little doors and a chandelier of original whale-oil lamps. It is a town landmark along with the imposing six-columned Old Whaling Church that dominates Main Street and now serves the community as a performing arts center, presenting plays and concerts.

Next door to the center is the home of Dr. Daniel Fisher, built by the richest man on the island. The enterprising doctor not only practiced medicine and manufactured hardtack for ships but also was the largest maker of spermaceti candles and holder of the contract to supply all the lighthouses in the country with whale oil.

Behind his home is the 1672 Vincent House, the oldest house on the island, with its original brickwork, hardware and woodwork intact, carefully preserved to show how buildings were constructed 300 years ago.

The 1765 Thomas Cooke House, now headquarters of the Dukes County Historical Society, holds collections of antique furniture, scrimshaw, ship models, costumes and gear used by the early residents on the island.

At the eastern end of the waterfront, the tiny ferry to Chappaquiddick Island comes and goes regularly, loading or discharging cars, passengers and bicycles.

Not far from Edgartown is the Place by the Wayside, marking the spot where Thomas Mayhew, Jr. often preached to the Indians and where they saw him for the last time. The stones the Indians placed on the spot in his memory were added to year by year and eventually cemented together as a memorial bearing a bronze marker.

Oak Bluffs

If Edgartown is a throwback to the whaling days of the 1800s, Oak Bluffs is vintage Victoriana. This gingerbread town was the spark that ignited the tourist boom on Martha's Vineyard.

Wesleyan Grove, the campground for the Methodist meeting in 1835, proved as much of

The imposing Old Whaling
Church bears witness to the wealth wrested
from the sea by the ships
that set out from Edgartown harbour.

Though the sea brought wealth to Edgartown from whaling and its oil and bone products, it also claimed its toll. Markers in the Burying Ground of the Federated Church are last reminders of many brave men who were lost at sea usually from the open dories which were often swamped by heavy seas and foundered.

The oldest house on Martha's Vineyard is the shingled Vincent House in Edgartown **right**, still carefully preserved with its original brickwork, hardware and woodwork intact after three centuries.

a lure to visitors as the meeting itself. More people came every year for the sunshine and sermons, each church group with its own communal tent where everyone bedded down in the straw that was readily available from local farmers. Eventually there were individual "family tents,"then cottages designed to look like tents. And as the cottages multiplied, they vied for the curliest curlicues and fanciest frills that were the Victorian style of the day. By the 1870s, as many as 30,000 attended the Illumination Night ceremonies that marked the end of the summer season with a show of Japanese lanterns and fireworks.

A high picket fence was built around the campgrounds to wall off such distractions as ocean beaches, fishing and walking in the woods, but to no avail. Wesleyan Grove became "Cottage City" and that grew into Ocean Grove, as steamboats continued to bring more visitors to play as well as pray. The horse cars that used to bring visitors from the docks to the Tabernacle were replaced by a steam railroad that went all the way to Katama. By 1879, the tent Tabernacle itself had given way to a new steel structure that still stands as a memento of the days of ironwork architecture. Electric trolleys soon arrived to supplant the steam train on the run from Vineyard Haven to Oak Bluff and then came the automobile, each improvement bringing more visitors.

Progress added galleries, shops, restaurants and antique stores on Circuit Avenue, but did little to alter the look of the town. Visitors still go down to Ocean Park, the semicircular green ringed by old wooden houses, for summer concerts in the octagonal bandstand on the green. The Flying Horses still twirl on what is believed to be the oldest carousel, a

Above The arching Chappaquiddick Bridge leads across Cape Pogue Bay to the Cape Pogue Wildlife Refuge and Wasque Reservation. This wild and solitary barrier beach and its expanses of dunes, salty marshes and thickets are a nesting area for thousands of birds.

Below left Fishing boats frame Edgartown harbor. In the distance the tiny Chappaquiddick ferry plies its way across the channel on the five-minute ride that brings visitors to the unspoiled beaches and untouched nature preserves of the neighbouring island.

Below right Almost hidden in the trees, Mayhew Chapel is named for Thomas Mayhew, Jr., who led the first settlement on Martha's Vineyard and brought Christianity to the native Indians. The simple chapel is the place where they worshipped.

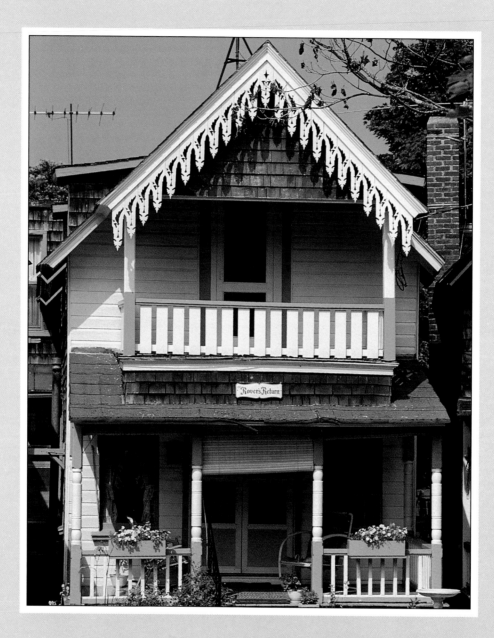

fixture in town since the 1870s, though the
motor these days is electric instead of the
steam-powered original. Along with horses,
the carousel boasts unique paintings of old
New England scenes and coastal views.

A Hansel and Gretel Museum of dolls and
doll furniture from the nineteenth century also
offers a bit of nostalgia for visitors young and
old.

In Trinity Park, the center of the Wesleyan
Grove meetings, the open air Tabernacle continues to hold summer services and concerts.
Trinity Methodist Church and a row of multi-
colored gingerbread Carpenter Gothic houses
also remain. The tall thin shape of the homes
and their narrow lots bear witness to the tents
that were the original occupants of these sites.
The Wesley House, the only remaining old
wooden hotel, is another reminder of the old
days.

Ocean Grove's colorful past still gives rise
to many festive events each year. The Camp-
meeting Association continues to dress its cottages with lanterns on Illumination Night in
mid-August, a band concert is held in the
Tabernacle and fireworks light the skies over
the waterfront as they did in the old days.
Tivoli Day in mid-September salutes the
town's Victorian heritage with bike and sail-
boat races, a street dance and block party on
Circuit Avenue and the blessing of the fishing
fleet.

The traditionally fine fishing in its waters
spawned a new Ocean Grove event in the
1940s that has grown into one of the largest
annual fishing events on the east coast, drawing fishermen from throughout the country.
Known as the Martha's Vineyard Striped Bass
and Blue Fish Derby, it is timed for the fall
migration of the large game fish to their breed-
ing grounds in the south and offers generous
rewards for prize catches.

West Tisbury

From Ocean Grove to West Tisbury is a return
from the Victorian era to a typical early New
England village, with white spired church,

general store and old mill. The presence of the mill was an early attraction since there was no stream in Edgartown that could be dammed for a water mill. In the 1840s, the grist mill became a mill for manufacturing fabric made from Island wool.

The stone walls that bound the first farms are very much in evidence in the West Tisbury countryside, and the village remains an agricultural center with the Fair Grounds that host the island's annual fair in late August, the scene of livestock contests, ox pulls, agricultural exhibits and old-fashioned fiddler's competitions. The Massachusetts Woodsman Competition at the Fair honors those who still boast prowess with the axe. For the days of the fair, Martha's Vineyard returns to the time when such fairs were the major social event of a summer season.

Some of West Tisbury's older homes started as inns to break the long trip from Island ports to Gay Head or Chilmark. Daniel Webster was a guest at the West Tisbury house next to the general store. The home across the pond was built by the son of Myles Standish in 1668. The big houses on Music Street were occupied by the wealthy sea captains of the town. The name came from the pianos they purchased with their profits.

Lambert's Cove, where the town's anchorage used to lie, has its own handsome homes and white church and a popular beach.

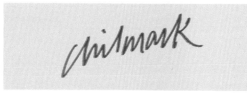

Along with North and West Tisbury and Gay Head, Chilmark is part of the quiet rural western portion of the island that the natives call "Up Island," areas of rolling hills, farmland and superb coastline that contain many of the finest summer homes. Some of the choicest beaches here are private, closely guarded by caretakers who make sure they are exclusively reserved for residents. Two of the most beautiful are Chilmark's Squibnocket and Lucy Vincent Beaches.

The island's early farming days are evidenced here in the old stone walls that ribbon

Lobster pots, fishermen's nets and shingled shanties, **left** and **overleaf**, make Menemsha's harbor unique on Martha's Vineyard, yet still a timeless symbol of the quintessential New England fishing village.

Menemsha harbor **right** still is called home by commercial fishing boats. Despite fierce currents, these craft maneuver in all weathers.

the hills, once used to prevent flocks of sheep from straying. The stone animal pound on the South Road was used to hold the strays, whose owners were fined for their carelessness in not keeping fence gates closed.

There are buildings from the past as well. The village school remains where it has stood for more than a century, even though the older children now attend the Regional High School. The painted steeple of the old church is "new"—added when the building was moved from its original site to the center of the village in 1915.

The grove known as Beetlebung Corner got its name from the islanders' nickname for the tupelo trees here, hardwood traditionally used for "Bungs" to plug the holes of barrels, casks and boats. It is a crossroads, the Middle Road providing sweeping views of farmland and ocean beyond, the North Road leading to the Menemsha, the only "Up Island"harbor.

Menemsha's harbor is filled with fishing boats who unload their catches here rather than make the extra mileage to the other side of the island. It is the best place on the island to buy seafood fresh from the catch. The fisherman's shacks, fishing nets and lobster traps look much as they might have a century ago, the timeless quintessential New England fishing village.

Before the Coast Guard station was built here, the residents watched out for each other with volunteer groups who took dories out into the storm to help fishermen in trouble. Some of the boats were kept at Squibnocket Landing, now a beach for town residents.

Gay Head

The westernmost tip of the island, windswept Gay Head is a landscape of dunes, moors and the famous clay cliffs. The cliffs are the evidence of the glacier's Ice Age visit to the island. The clays and sediments it left behind are now waving layers of sand, gravel and clay in yellow, red and orange hues descending to the water's edge. Each layer tells of a different era

in the development of the ancient coastal plain. Buried forests are the stripes of black near the bottom, iron and other minerals are the stains of yellow and red. At sunset, all the colors deepen to a luminous glow. The lighthouse here was one of the first revolving lighthouses in the country when it was built in 1799.

The clay was prized for pottery-making by the Wampanoags and for brickmaking by early settlers. Later it was shipped back to be used by potters on shore. As erosion chips away at the cliffs, the clay sometimes yields fossils of vanished animals and ancient whales who once inhabited the island and its waters. In the gravel layers near the top, whale bones and sharks' teeth are common, and bits of the skeletons of a camel and wild horse have been uncovered. Though the town prohibits digging in the cliffs, beach walkers with a keen eye may find fossils washed out by the rain.

Once upon a time, Gay Head's Indians were known for their skill as courageous seamen noted among the whaling fleet for their proficiency as "boatsteerers," those who put the iron into the whale. Many Indians remain in Gay Head, today mostly in evidence for their wares in gift shops placed at the cliff path to catch the busloads of tourists who come to see the island's most interesting geological site.

Beauty Spots

The cliffs are only one of the marks of the glacier. Old House Pond and Fresh Pond are kettle-hole ponds and Great Pond is a glacial

The U.S. Coast Guard Station at Menemsha **above left** now provides the service that residents once supplied for each other — standing watch and sending help for fishermen in trouble at sea.

The Gay Head Light **below** was one of the most important on the Atlantic Coast and one of the nation's first revolving lighthouses.

A sanctuary for birds and wildlife as well as man, Cedar Tree Neck **center** is one of many protected areas on Martha's Vineyard where a walk through the brush rewards with stunning ocean views.

stream dammed up by later walls of sand.

All contribute to the variety of the landscape and the beauty spots on the island's many lush acres and miles of shore that are treasured by those who know it best. Despite recent island development, preservationists have helped to keep these areas inviolate to be enjoyed by visitors today as well as future generations.

Twelve conservation areas comprising some 5,000 acres are set aside to remain as woodland, pond, marsh and shore; many individual landowners add to that total every year. The Hough family began a foundation with part of their own land in 1959, and when Jacqueline Kennedy Onassis purchased 378 acres at Gay Head in 1978, she pledged also to keep "this irreplaceable fragment of a vanishing island" as a wildlife sanctuary.

Miles of paved bike paths in the state forest help tourists to discover the island's beauty spots, particularly in the State Forest and on the paved path from Oak Bluffs to Edgartown.

State Forest

The center of Martha's Vineyard has been set aside as forestland and over the past two decades replanted with pines now grown tall to blend with the oaks. It is crisscrossed with hiking and biking trails to make its tranquil shaded beauty accessible and to provide for travel between Vineyard Haven, Oak Bluffs, Edgartown and West Tisbury.

Trustees of the Reservation

The Trustees of the Reservation is the oldest private foundation on the island dedicated to

preservation. It maintains four properties. The Cape Pogue Wildlife Refuge and Wasque Reservation, 489 and 200 acres respectively, are the largest of their holdings. They are on Chappaquiddick Island, reached by the tiny ferry boat that makes the short run from Edgartown.

These two fragile areas of barrier beach form the northeastern corner of the island, a wild expanse of scrub flats, dunes and thickets providing a variety of water habitats in salt marshes, ponds and tidal flats. As a stopover and refuge for migratory birds and nesting grounds for shore birds, the beach here is visited by thousands of winged creatures each year. It is open to beaching and fishing and to four-wheel vehicles by permit.

The 580-acre Trustees property known as Long Point on the south shore of the island in West Tisbury includes Long Pond, Tisbury Great Pond, Middle Point Cove, Long Cove and a half mile of South Beach on the Atlantic. The variety of habitats from freshwater to salt-water pond to ocean makes it another haven for birds—and bird watchers.

Menemsha Hills Reservation protects part of the sand cliff and the pebbled and boul-dered beach in front of it. The 149-acre prop-erty is off to itself, a three-quarter-mile walk from the parking lot.

Northern Cardinal This bright red-crested bird is America's most spectacular finch. It can be seen in gardens and woodland edges.

Formed by Henry and Betty Hough to "pre-serve, administer and maintain natural habi-tats for wild life on Martha's Vineyard," the foundation now owns more than 750 acres of pristine island property.

One of the areas it maintains is Cedar Tree Neck, off Indian Hill Road on the north shore, 250 acres combining a bird and wildlife sanctu-ary with memorable views and the chance to swim, fish and picnic. A walk beneath shady trees leads gradually uphill through silver birches and a carpet of woodland ferns, mosses and mushrooms. A beach at the over-look atop a 30-foot bluff invites a stop to con-template the seaside panorama.

Center Nantucket harbor, the scene of constant activity by day, settles into scenic repose with the setting of the sun.

Felix Neck Wildlife Sanctuary

Woods and wildflowers and open country down to the salt marshes comprise the 200 acres of this property run by the Felix Neck Wildlife Trust, an affiliate of the Massachusetts Audubon Society. A reptile pond, six miles of trails, exhibit centers and a library are part of the complex which is another important sanctuary for bird life. There is an observation hut for identifying and a photography blind to photograph the many species of wild ducks and geese.

Island Beaches

For many, the most beautiful of all Martha's Vineyard vistas are her beaches. While some of the best are private, there are enough prime public shorelands left to please the most ardent beach lovers, from the shallow protected areas on the north and east to the crashing surf on the south.

South Beach at Edgartown has been called the finest beach in America, with its three wide miles of powder sand with surf on one side, protected pond on the other. Easily reached in summer by shuttle bus from Edgartown, it is the most popular of the island beaches. The state beach between Oak Bluffs and Edgartown is also public, along with the protected Lighthouse Beach at Starbuck's Neck in Edgartown, overlooking the harbor. The water laps gently here, as it does at Menemsha's Public Beach, another beach open to everyone.

Even day-trippers can take advantage of the beaches in Oak Bluffs and Vineyard Haven, but for escapists, it is the dunes and tall beach grasses at Wasque Point on Chappaquiddick that appeal, with its shores of great unspoiled natural beauty and relative solitude. Also within a nature preserve is the fine beach at Long Point.

Among the beaches available only to residents, Lambert's Cove on the north shore in West Tisbury provides sugar-fine sand and calm clear water with sailboats tacking off-shore in Vineyard Sound adding to the view. In Chilmark, Lucy Vincent Beach, beneath the bluffs with outcroppings of dark clay, is another favorite of "up islanders" and Squib-nocket Beach provides pounding surf for swimmers and soothing sound for sunbathers.

Public and private, sheltered and wave-splashed, like most of Martha's Vineyard, the beaches offer diversity and something for everyone.

Canada Goose Familiar to Americans across the country, this goose is characteristically to be seen flying with others in a 'v' formation.

Growth vs Preservation

When a 45-minute ferry ride is all that separates the mainland from an island of tremendous popular appeal, the problems are obvious. Martha's Vineyard swells in summer from 10,000 to 70,000 residents, a number compounded by uncounted hordes of day-trippers. There are many who want to build to take advantage of the island's drawing power, and town meetings are frequently battlegrounds between condominium builders and developers and islanders determined to restrict growth to protect the open spaces and repose that winter and summer people alike treasure.

Perhaps symbolic of the struggle the island faces was a recent would-be developer who is a great-grandson of Herman Melville. A full-page ad in the *Vineyard Gazette* begged him to remember his ancestor's commitment to nature.

How to allow growth without despoiling nature or spoiling the island? Nature preserves are one answer, but the entire island cannot be put under wraps. It is a problem that zoners and planners debate daily, as an island kingdom of beaches, pasture and woodland, of clapboard houses and fishing boats fights to retain its heritage.

Nor is Martha's Vineyard alone with its dilemma. Its neighbor, Nantucket, faces some of the same problems 30 miles out to sea.

NANTUCKET

*A*nd thus have these naked Nantucketers, these sea-hermits, issuing from their anthill in the sea, overrun and conquered the world like so many Alexanders..."

So wrote Herman Melville in *Moby Dick*, describing the little island 30 miles from shore whose whaling fleet was largely responsible for the oil that lit the lamps of the world. Today the town of Nantucket is in many ways remarkably unchanged from its early days as a whaling capital, its cobbled streets, seaman's cottages and sea captain's mansions comprising America's largest living Colonial town. Nantucket Island occupies a unique niche in history, and a walk through Nantucket town is an exceptional stroll back in time.

Nor is the timeless town the only part of Nantucket that still matches the meaning of the name given by the Indians long ago, "the faraway island." Outside of town, much of the land remains a world of low-lying, wide-open and untamed heather-covered moors, bound on all sides by extraordinary expanses of beach and water—rough and rolling Atlantic surf on the south shore, calm warm waters of Nantucket Sound to the north and miles of solitary seashore for wandering on every side.

Here, too, conservationists battle daily with developers to preserve this irreplaceable open space, and while parts of the island are undeniably changing, for the most part its singular wild beauty remains undisturbed, a rare respite from the workaday real world across the water.

Those who love the island debate which is her finest season. Spring arrives in a rush of blue skies and golden daffodils, celebrated with a local festival and a spate of freshly painted picket fences and shutters. Pearly blossoms of beach plum and blackberry transform the winter brown of the moors. Summer's sunshine and breezes are relished by beach-goers, bikers, kite flyers and sailors, while some await the lingering warmth of silent autumn days when the crowds are gone and cranberries and heather put a rosy glow over the entire island.

At holiday time, Nantucket takes on a Dickensian air. The cobblestones along Main Street to the harbor are raised to make room for the planting of live Christmas trees bordering the street on both sides and the old-

Right and **overleaf** A two-hour journey into the past on the Nantucket Ferry brings passengers to the cobbled Main Street and charming residential areas of America's largest living Colonial town.

Opposite Nantucket's intrepid whalers became the wonder of the seas. At one time over 100 Nantucket vessels were abroad, battling waves and whales to provide the oil that lit the lamps of the world.

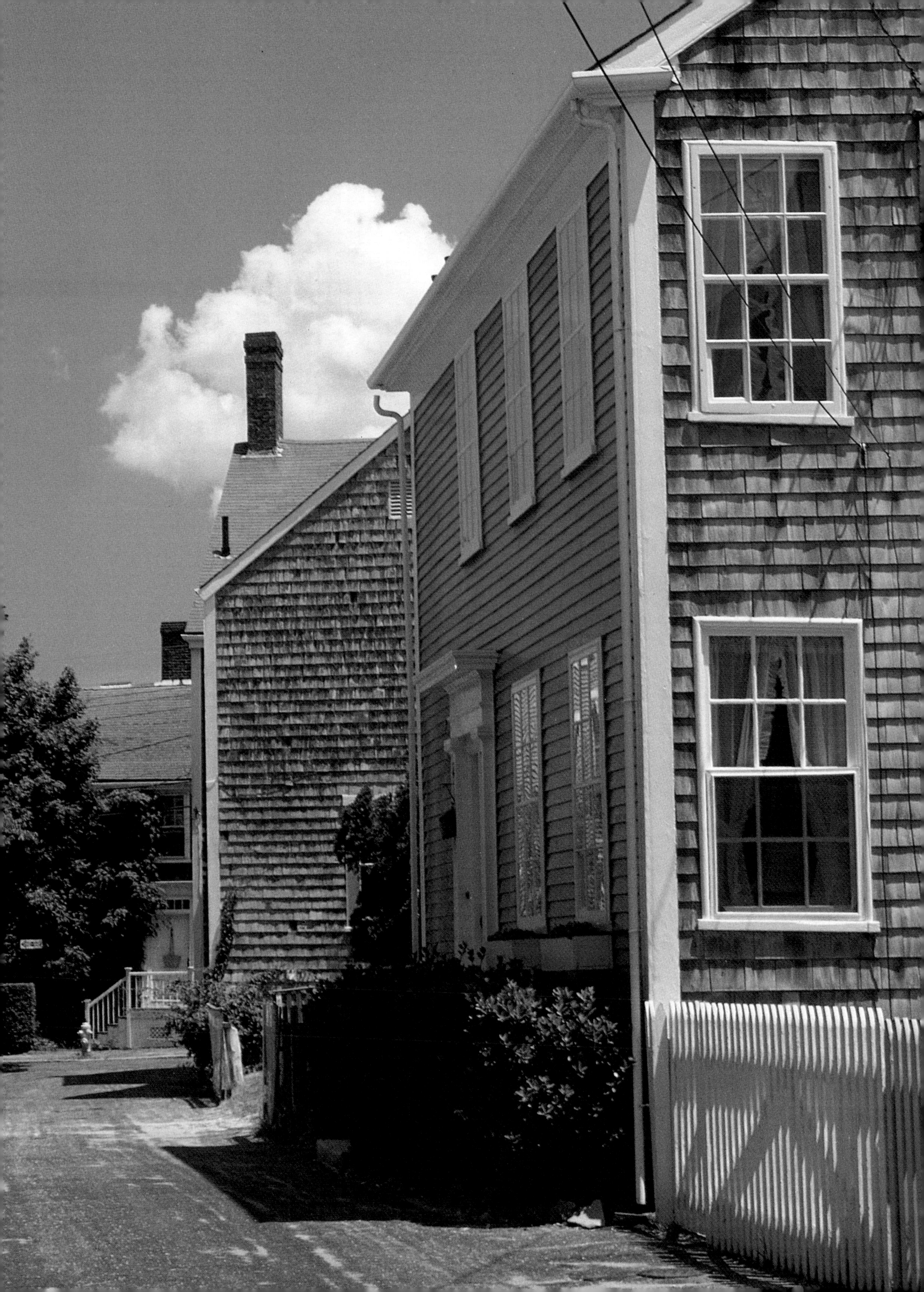

fashioned street lights are festooned with greenery and red ribbons. Schoolchildren trim the trees with cranberries, painted shells and other native island decorations.

On the second Saturday in December, the annual Christmas stroll means hot mulled cider and roasted chestnuts, candles in the windows, carolers, minstrels and the arrival of Santa Claus via horse-drawn sleigh.

Even in the gray days of winter, snow gives a special serenity to the island, old inns burn cozy and welcoming blazes in the fireplace and there is time to reflect on the island's beauty without distractions.

At any season, Nantucket is a travel experience as unique as its singular history.

Early History

In the beginning, Nantucket's story paralleled that of Cape Cod and Martha's Vineyard—

Seamen's cottages **left**, snug captains' quarters **right** and the mansions of wealthy shipowners **center** remind of a time when Nantucket's fleet was responsible for much of world's supply of whale oil.

formed by the glaciers, first mentioned in official records by the same Bartholomew Gosnold who had given the Cape and the Vineyard their names. Another Englishman, George Weymouth, first described the white sandy cliffs of Sankaty Head sighted from his ship in 1605, though rough waters kept him from going ashore.

The island had been occupied for many unrecorded years by the Algonquin Indians. It was part of the large region from the coast of Maine to New York that was claimed by the English and given out to favorites at court. Nantucket was first given to Lord Sterling, who seemed to take little interest in his holding in the middle of the sea, since his agent sold Nantucket in 1641 to the Watertown, Massachusetts, merchant, Thomas Mayhew, who also acquired Martha's Vineyard and the Elizabeth Islands in that same £40 transaction. Mayhew wanted the land as a grazing place for his flocks, but according to records he did not pursue this idea, and the Indians remained the sole occupants of the island for another 18 years. Mayhew sold the rights to Nantucket in 1659 for £30 and "two beaver hats, one for myself and one for my wife." The nine partici-

Right Nantucket harbor with its carefully restored wharves and cottages retains the look of an early American seafaring town, adding to its appeal as one of New England's favorite vacation destinations.

pants in the transaction are names still familiar on the island: Tristram Coffin and his son Peter, Thomas Macy, Christopher Hussey, Richard Swain, Thomas Barnard, Stephen Greenleaf, John Swain and William Pike. Mayhew did wisely retain a share of all lands and privileges for himself.

To encourage more people to join the new settlement, each of the purchasers was allowed to choose another partner for the venture, and more familiar Nantucket names joined the rolls: Nathaniel and Edward Starbuck, Tristram Coffin, Jr., Thomas Look, James Coffin, John Smith, Robert Barnard, Robert Pike and Thomas Coleman. Another 14 half-shares went to craftsmen whose skills would be needed on the island—a carpenter, joiner, miller, shoemaker, tailor and seaman among others. Among these men were Edward Cartwright, Captain John Gardner and Peter Foulger, who would later become the grandfather of Benjamin Franklin.

Each share entitled the owner to 1/27 of the island, excepting the holdings of Mayhew. The shareholders became members of the "Proprietors of the Common and Undivided Lands of Nantucket." However, dissension was to follow later when the half-share men demanded equal rights and say in island affairs.

The newcomers chose this remote new homeland to escape the strict religious rule of the Puritans in Massachusetts. Thomas Macy of Salisbury and his wife and children were the first actually to settle on the island, bringing with them Edward Starbuck and 12-year-old Isaac Coleman. Macy had been fined for allowing Quakers to take shelter from a rainstorm in his home, an act considered an offense in a community that had no tolerance for the Society of Friends. Unknown to Macy, Quakers later were to play a major role on Nantucket. He himself was to become the patriarch of a long line of Macys, including Rowland Hussey Macy, whose little store in Manhattan grew to be the largest department store in the world.

Thanks to the good relations built by Mayhew, Macy was greeted cordially by the Indians, which probably helped him to survive his first long and lonely winter. According to Mayhew's terms, the settlers had promised to repurchase their land parcels from the Indians. Macy had first settled in what is now Madaket, an area now known for its sunsets and pounding surf. As more families arrived in the spring they moved to more hospitable land surrounding the small sheltered harbor of what is now Capaum Pond, on the north shore. By the end of the year, there were 60 people living in the settlement they called Sherburne, and the settlement had expanded eastward along the Cliff and toward Hummock Pond.

The settlers got along well with the natives, who taught their new neighbors how to farm, fish and hunt in their new environs. However, the Indians had no knowledge of what "selling" meant, and expected to share the land with the settlers. They learned too late they had forfeited the right to their own grazing and farmlands. And their numbers began to decrease rapidly, not so much from mistreatment by the settlers as from the new diseases they brought.

According to one early account, "the Indians [on Nantucket] were not extirpated by fraud, violence or injustice as has been the case in so many provinces. On the contrary, they have been treated by the people as brethren." By 1854, the last male Indian with Nantucket blood died at the age of 82, and the following year Dorcas Honorable, the last full-blooded Indian female, also passed away.

There were some political problems for the new settlement. Charles II had given a grant to his brother, the Duke of York, that included Nantucket and brought it under the governorship of New York, and the islanders had to repurchase their patent with an annual payment of four barrels of codfish. The settlement was officially incorporated at this time, the year 1673, under the name of Sherburne. It was returned to the authority of the Bay Colony of Massachusetts in 1692.

Meanwhile, on the island, the half-share men had begun their battle for equal representation in island government, led in their fight by Captain John Gardner and Peter Foulger. The issue was greater than parcels of land; it involved the principle of democracy on the island, and Thomas Macy and other full shareholders supported the movement. Tristram Coffin and his sons and sons-in-law, who included Nathaniel Starbuck, were leaders of the opposing faction, the landed gentry who were for the status quo. Two years of controversy went by and Foulger, who was the Clerk of the Court, went to jail for refusing to

give up Court records to Coffin, before the Governor took sides with the "half-shares" and appointed John Gardner as Chief Magistrate.

The rift was healed some years later after Tristram Coffin's death when his grandson, Jethro, married Gardner's daughter, uniting the two factions. As a wedding present, the Coffins donated wood from their sawmill and Gardner donated land on Sunset Hill for a home for the couple. That house, now maintained by the Nantucket Historical Association, is known as the island's Oldest House and is open to the public in the summer. It is also known to residents as the "Horseshoe House", and is of great interest to architectural buffs for its huge center chimney and enormous fireplaces, the heavy ships knees used in its construction and the so-called "Indian Closet."

Tristram Coffin remained a major force on Nantucket, however, through his prolific descendants. In 1880, more than 500 Coffins gathered for a family reunion. It is said that there are over 10,000 Coffins on the island and the mainland who can trace their lineage to Tristram.

Gardner left his own prodigious line of descendants. The names Coffin, Gardner, Swain, Hussey, Meader, Worth, Coleman, Folger, Macy and Starbuck can still be seen today on shops and business listings on Nantucket. They are the real Nantucketers, direct descendants of the rugged settlers who developed the island.

The victory of Gardner's and Foulger's forces determined the future course of the island as a democratic, free-thinking society and set the stage for what was to follow.

The Quakers

A typical wooden Nantucket house built in 1758.

For some time, the settlers, who had fled the mainland seeking religious freedom, adopted no formal religion. Then traveling Quaker missionaries found a convert in Mary Coffin Starbuck, who began in 1708 to hold a monthly Meeting of Friends in her home. The Quaker

Once a major whaling port,
Nantucket is now more famous for its
pleasure craft than for commercial
fishing boats.

Left Guarding the entrance to Nantucket harbor is Brant Point Lighthouse, once a familiar sight to whalers, now a landmark for ferry passengers and the many sailors, yachtsmen and fishermen who frequent the harbor. The original lighthouse placed here in 1746 was the second ever constructed on the coast of Colonial America.

philosophy of personal freedom and pacifism appealed to the independent islanders, and the religion was rapidly accepted. Within a short time, the first Quaker Meeting House was built, and soon Quakerism became the guiding tenet in Nantucket life. No other American community had such a large proportion of Quakers in its population. Strong believers in the importance of education, it was the Quakers who were the first to establish schools that were open to all on Nantucket. Quaker thrift and industry were to be major contributors to the glory days of whaling ahead.

Off to Sea

The earliest Nantucketers tried farming the sandy land, but it was a fruitless effort and they began to look to the sea for their livelihood. Emulating the Indians, they began using the carcasses of dead whales washed up on the shore to refine the blubber into oil for their lamps. Then they began whaling near the shore in small boats manned in part or entirely by Indians. Shore whaling was a major industry until the middle of the 1700s, when the scarcity of nearby whales ended its profitability.

One story goes that the idea of deep-sea whaling began with a 1712 storm that blew a captain out to sea, where he came upon a school of valuable sperm whales and managed to harpoon one. Another says that it was in 1690 that a sloop master sighted a whale whose spouting indicated that it was a different species, and it was killing this whale that marked the discovery that the spermaceti whale contained great quantities of finest quality oil stored in its great head.

Whatever the beginning, Nantucket's location 30 miles out to sea made it much closer to the migratory routes of the sperm whales than Cape Cod whalers. Deep-sea whaling in larger vessels developed into a new industry that was to bring enormous wealth to the island. It was perilous work, but with great rewards. Just before the Revolutionary War, nearly 100

Nantucket vessels were plying the seas, bringing home for sale the whalebone in demand for canes, umbrellas and corset stays, oil for lamps, sperm candles and the valuable ambergris, worth up to 50 dollars an ounce for use in the preparation of fine perfume.

The center of island activity moved to the harbor-front, where warehouses, candle factories, chandleries, coopers, rope walks, shipsmiths shops and blacksmiths fashioning strong and sharp harpoons appeared along the wharves being built on the "Great Harbor." The town rapidly increased in size from 1680 to 1725. Many of the first Sherburne settlers moved closer to the harbor, and North, Centre, State and Duke Streets were laid out. The first permanent wharf, Straight Wharf, was built in 1723 by the Macys, as islanders began to sell directly to London, bypassing Boston merchants. Nantucket trade expanded to the West Indies, France, Holland and Spain. As the whaling enterprise prospered, Old South wharf was built in 1740, Old North in 1750, New North in 1770 and Commercial Wharf in 1790.

One reason a small and isolated island was able to establish such a major world port was the tight-knit makeup of Nantucket society. Hard-working Quakers were known for their conscientious attention to business. Because they did not believe in ostentatious living, they were able to accumulate wealth. Many of the wealthiest shipowners and merchants were Friends. Intermarriage and the influence of the church knit close ties among the founding families and strong loyalties and cooperation in their endeavors. Local tradesmen produced most of the goods needed to supply the whalers. The ships themselves were all but self-sufficient, able to boil down their catch on board and have oil ready for trade without need of outside assistance or middlemen merchants.

A Woman's Place

The respect the Quakers held for all men could be seen in their treatment of women. As Nan-

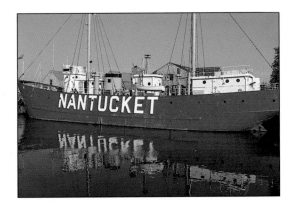

Though pleasure boats **above left** and **center** now occupy the area where great whaling enterprises once prospered, Nantucket is still a seafaring town. The waterfront remains the heart of island activity.

Nantucket lightships **above right** were stationed 20 miles or more out to sea in the 1800s to warn shipping away from treacherous shoals. Crews whiling away long hours aboard produced the island's present best-known craft, sturdy Nantucket lightship baskets.

Nantucket sleighride The seas around Nantucket are sometimes very rough, as is shown in this early engraving.

tucket's whaling industry grew, there were many lonely wives left behind for weeks and even years at a time. It has been estimated that at any time during the whaling years the women on the island outnumbered the men by as many as four to one. The wives reared the children, managed the family finances, did the heavy chores and taught the boys until they were 12 years old and turned over to the more masculine tutelage of the whalers.

Of necessity, most Nantucket girls and women were unable to assume the usual dependent feminine role of the times. It was only natural that the women began assuming a role in community affairs as well as in their homes. They developed strong minds and wills and several kinds of leaders emerged.

Mary Coffin Starbuck was primarily responsible for the island becoming the foremost settlement of Quakers in the world when she converted to the faith at age 56 and convinced most of her neighbors to follow her.

Kesiah Coffin was the first successful businesswoman on the island. Her most fruitful venture came during the Revolutionary War when she told the British that most of the islanders were Tories like herself and convinced them to permit her vessels to continue trade with New York. This gave her a virtual monopoly during a period when no one else could get through even with daily necessities of living. Coffin took advantage of her position to overcharge her neighbors, and was rewarded by being deserted by her customers and ruined when normal trade resumed.

Lucretia Mott, an early feminist and a woman devoted to humanitarian causes, was a leader in the suffrage movement, while Anna Gardner was an early antislavery exponent who helped organize a convention on Nantucket where Frederick Douglass made his debut as a public speaker. After the Civil War, she went to the South to become one of the first teachers of freed slaves, returning to the island a few years before she died to publish a volume of poetry.

Perhaps the best known of the island's pioneering women was Maria Mitchell, the daughter of a mathematician, who seemed to have inherited a natural ability for astronomy. She gained international renown when she discovered a new comet on the night of October 1, 1847. Her discovery earned her a gold medal from the king of Denmark and the distinction of becoming the first woman Fellow of the Academy of Arts and Science, an honor no other woman would win for 100 years.

Other Nantucket women made their own contributions in their own ways. Rachel Bunker, when she died in 1795 at the age of 80, could claim 12 children, 122 grandchildren and 93 great-grandchildren, and had assisted at the births of some 3,000 of her neighbor's children.

Ups and Downs at Sea

Nantucket's burgeoning whaling industry was devastated by the Revolutionary War. Nantucket retained her Quaker neutrality, but at a terrible price. Distrusted by both sides, the islanders suffered heavy losses. According to local accounts, 1,200 seamen out of a total population under 7,000 were either captured by the English or perished in the war. Of the 100 whaling and 50 merchant vessels owned by islanders before the war, 134 fell into enemy hands and another 15 were lost by shipwreck. The cost was over 1 million dollars in an era when a man's daily wage was about 70 cents.

But the sturdy islanders rebounded. In 1783, the first American flag ever sailed into a British port was displayed on the ship *Bedford*, laden with whale oil from Nantucket. In 1791, the whaleship *Beaver* rounded the Horn and opened the Pacific to whaling. Two of the buildings on Main Street, the Pacific National Bank and the Pacific Club, bear witness to the period when Nantucket ships charted new paths around the world. Only whaling masters who had sailed the Pacific were eligible for the club.

By 1793, the fleet was back to 30 vessels ranging the world; on the island there were 5,000 inhabitants and almost 600 houses. By the early 1800s, there were another 2,000 residents, 850 homes, four churches and scores of shops and tradesmen.

The War of 1812 with its British naval blockades was another setback, and there was

A resident offers
a personal welcome to spring.

Top left A typical sea captain's mansion on Nantucket's cobbled lanes, with an arched fan light over the door and a 'widow's walk' above, named for the wives who used these balconies to watch anxiously for the safe return of their husbands from the sea.

Nantucket's shingled cottages and cobbled streets were preserved by a quirk of fate — economic hard times that prevented the islanders from modernizing their homes **preceding page** and **right**. When summer roses ramble over fences and trellises and planters burst into color, the 'little gray lady of the sea' blooms into an island beauty.

competition from the rising ports of New Bedford, New London and Sag Harbor, yet the hardy Nantucket whalers continued to survive and to prosper. The height of Nantucket's prosperity came in the 1840s. Shipowners built the stately mansions on Upper Main Street; whaling captains lived in the fine homes on Orange Street.

Then disaster struck. A devastating fire destroyed the waterfront in 1846. Though rebuilding was rapid, the gold rush of 1849 tempted many islanders to leave to seek their fortunes elsewhere. Among them was R.H. Macy, who left his father's store to go west, but who was to find his fortune not in the gold fields but in the store he would later found in New York City. The original Macy family store can still be seen on Main Street.

The coming Civil War was first felt on Nantucket in 1822. Slaves brought to the island in 1770 had been freed and lived peacefully on Nantucket in a section of town near upper Pleasant Street that was known as "New Guinea." Among them were newcomers Arthur Cooper and his family, who had

escaped from Virginia via the Underground Railroad and made their way to Nantucket. When the Coopers' owners heard of their whereabouts, they sent lawmen and a slave-catcher to return the Coopers to Virginia.

When they arrived, the party found a crowd of blacks waiting for them, along with a large number of Nantucketers. Judge Walter Folger told them that Massachusetts law did not recognize slavery and that he would arrest anyone who tried to molest the Coopers. While the intruders argued that federal law took precedence, Oliver Gardner quietly made off with the Coopers, disguised them in Quaker clothing and took them to his home; where they remained hidden for six weeks. The spirit of the islanders was too much for the Southerners, and they left without accomplishing their mission.

When war broke out, it took more men away from Nantucket. The fleet dwindled further when its profits were taken away by the discovery of petroleum in 1859. The last bark sailed in 1869; the glory days of Nantucket whaling were over.

Old lamp posts and lush summer foliage bedeck a charming Nantucket home.

Often hidden behind garden walls, Nantucket cottages are built of traditional and natural materials, clapboard, pine and oak.

Preserved by Poverty

Ironically, it was hard times that preserved Nantucket's original architecture. The island went into serious decline in the late 1800s, its wharves and homes in disrepair, the population down from a high of 20,000 to a struggling 2,000.

Poverty meant that no one could afford to "modernize," so while the rest of the mainland was changing, Nantucket remained untouched.

Then came the first stirrings of a saving source of income as it was discovered that this beach-rimmed island was an ideal vacation spot. Nantucket had been a port of call for packets and merchant vessels for years. Now the boats began bringing summer people. Houses could be bought for a pittance and building was cheap. Large hotels, only one of which survives, went up around the island at Brant Point, the Cliff, 'Sconset, Surfside and

Cobbled streets in Nantucket
town **left** and **above** are the happy result of
'hard times' that left the
island too poor to modernize. It was the
untouched Colonial look
of the town along with its beaches that
eventually brought it new
prosperity from tourism.

Shingled cottages along Nantucket's wharves **opposite**, many now converted to shops and galleries, were carefully restored to maintain their original look. The sleek craft at the piers **above** and **below** bear little resemblance to the whaling ships that once took shelter here.

Wauwinet. Islanders living in the great old houses began opening them to paying guests. The island economy was also aided by the discovery that the Nantucket bay scallop was a delicacy much desired by the rest of the world.

The old spirit of enterprise speeded things along. A city water supply was laid, electric lights were introduced, a narrow-gauge steam railroad was built in 1881 and extended to the end of the island to 'Sconset a few years later. Nantucket greeted the twentieth century as a modernized island. Only one new invention was banned—the automobile. It was not allowed on the island until 1918, when the ban was lifted by a margin of only 40 votes, much to the regret of many islanders.

A New Golden Era

Two world wars and the Depression had slowed island development, but it took giant strides forward in the 1960s when a wealthy summer resident, Walter Beinecke, formed a corporation named Sherburne, after the original Island settlement, and set out to rescue and renovate the decaying wharves. Sherburne went on to acquire large portions of island real estate and to take over and renovate some of the better hotels.

Visitors to Straight Wharf today find the area pre-served with a cobblestone mall, old gaslights and weathered, gray-shingled cottages with the same small-paned windows and white trim of the typical island buildings. They are reproductions built to maintain the

W H I R L Y G I G S

Whimsical whirligigs
made by early carvers to turn in the
ever-present Cape
Cod breezes are prize pieces of folk
art today. Replicas
of the originals can be seen in
motion on lawns
throughout the Cape and roadside
stands offer them as
prized souvenirs for visitors.

Nantucket Lightship was for years the beacon guarding the infamous Nantucket Shoals. Stationed at the head of the shoals in the storm tossed Atlantic, the Lightship kept merchant ships from foundering in the rock strewn shallows, long a graveyard for landward bound vessels.

character of the town and the center today for art galleries, gift shops and restaurants. Boats of all sizes and shapes fill the harbor and ferry boats bring a seemingly unceasing stream of visitors from the mainland.

Moored at the wharf is one of the famous Nantucket lightships that were stationed off the island in the 1800s to protect trans-Atlantic ships from the treacherous shoal waters around the island. The first ship was stationed 24 miles out to sea in 1856.

Lightship Baskets

The long months of duty at sea of the lightship crews gave rise to one of Nantucket's best known products, the lightship baskets woven by the seaman to while away the time. Though they shared the old Indian technique of using long thin strips of wood called splints as material, these baskets were noted for their sturdiness, which came from borrowing some of the techniques of Nantucket coopers engaged in the making of barrels and casks. The baskets had board bottoms, vertical splints and circular binding hoops at the top. Bottoms for the first baskets were made of pine; later sycamore, black walnut and mahogany were used. Wood was at such a premium on Nantucket that the bottoms of old cigar boxes were sometimes used.

The early baskets were irregular in shape, but eventually blocks were developed, often cut from old spars from the ship. The baskets were shaped bottom-up on the blocks. The making of baskets kept the crew occupied and produced an original Nantucket craft. After World War II, a Filipino craftsman named José Reyes came to Nantucket and created a new kind of basket with a top made of mahogany. Next came ivory whales as ornaments for the top; Reyes had begun a new form of basket that became enormously popular as a hand-bag. The carefully crafted handmade baskets are expensive, but are unique to the island and a favorite souvenir for Nantucket visitors. They can be seen in many local shops.

The Nathaniel Macy House
on Walnut Lane, now open to the public, was
built in 1723. Inside are
the original fireplaces, fine furniture and
cooking utensils of the
period.

The baskets are an example that old and new, tradition and progress, are managing to coexist on Nantucket.

A Stroll Through the Park

Careful ordinances are now responsible for maintaining the extraordinary architecture of Nantucket town and controlling the look of new construction. The simple weathered rose-covered cottages of the Quakers remain, along with the mansions, and despite the tourist influx, church steeples remain the tallest structures on the island. It takes only a walk through town to transport a visitor back to the people and events of the past, beginning with the cobblestones that seem so picturesque today but were originally put down for purely practical reasons—to keep heavy oil drays from sinking into the mud.

At the corner of Main and Fair is the store where R.H. Macy gave up his first storekeeping job with his father to go whaling. Further on Main are the brick mansions of the ship-owning Coffins aboard whose vessel, *Charles and Mary*, Herman Melville once went to sea. The Coffin family was responsible for planting the stately elms on Main Street as well as bringing back the pines, larches and heather that have spread throughout the island landscape.

A few doors down on Walnut Lane, the Nathaniel Macy home is now open to the public. Next comes one of Nantucket's most noted sections—12 magnificent whaling mansions of various members of the Coffin and Starbuck families. The row of three brick-columned Starbuck mansions is seen in countless Nantucket photographs.

More historic homes await at every turn. There is the home where Maria Mitchell, the famous early female astronomer, was born and the observatory named for her. There are several residences and monuments to the Folger family, including a memorial to Abiah Folger, wife of Josiah Franklin and mother of Benjamin Franklin. Facing Main on Pleasant, the Hadwen-Satler mansion with a beautiful

garden in the rear has been maintained for the public by the Nantucket Garden Club. The 1723 Macy-Christian house on Liberty Street can also be visited. It is furnished with charming period furniture.

More homes recall the early names on the island; the Isaac Macy home, the home of Obed Macy, the island's first historian, and the home built by Job Macy in 1750. According to the story, his strict Quaker father refused to enter this two-story home, declaring it was too showy. There are three houses built by John Coleman and the home of Walter Folger, Jr., and his family of ten, a man who was considered an island genius, "one of the many curious-minded Folgers who descended from Peter Folger, the most notable being Benjamin Franklin," says a local brochure. "The islanders called them 'faculized Folgers.' Walter never had to earn a living. He was a mathematician, surveyor and astronomer, but his interest in science carried him into social relations and he served in the town as selectman and on the school boards and in trade and commercial organizations. He also became a lawyer, judge and representative both in Massachusetts legislature and the National Congress." Peter would have been proud.

Still another prominent Folger descendant lived in the Tupper home built in 1828 by Thomas Folger. His son, Charles James, became Secretary of the Treasury under President Arthur in 1881.

Orange Street is of particular note as the street that was the address of some 126 ships' captains.

Not all of Nantucket's interesting historic structures are houses. The Cooperage is a place where large and small oil casks were made in whaling days and the Old Gaol, a curious little building of square logs held by iron rods, has four little cells, one of them with a fireplace, that once held wrongdoers. A few steps beyond is the Old Burial Ground, a field where 5,000 Quakers are buried in rows, their graves unmarked in Quaker tradition. The Friends Meeting House on Fair Street, a stark gray-shingled building built in 1846, is the only remaining Quaker meetinghouse on the island.

The Old North Church Cemetery is the place to see the finely carved headstones of the eighteenth century. The creators of these stones used known symbols and their own

Many-hued Colonial homes make a stroll through Nantucket an architectural delight. The cobbles that seem so picturesque today were put down originally as a practical measure to keep heavy drays from sinking into the mud.

Nantucket's old gaol **above**
and **left** was built of square oak logs sheaved
with pine and shingled. It held
four cells for prisoners, one with the
undoubtedly welcome luxury
of a fireplace, but the peaceful annals of the
island record few wrongdoers
who resided here.

This original Nantucket
house has been
successfully converted by
the addition of large
windows and is now named
'Greater Light'. **right**

designs to make portraits, carved wings and stylized flowers, humanizing touches which brought out some remarkable sculpting during the Colonial and post-Revolutionary periods. The carving is an art form that flowered early and disappeared.

A few other points of interest are the First Coffin School, "founded for Coffins only," at the corner of Fair Street, built by Sir Isaac Coffin, a direct descendant of Tristram, before the advent of public education on the island, and the Old Mill on Sunset Hill, an island landmark, the only remaining one of four windmills that once turned on the island.

The Old Mill

The Old Mill is one of Nantucket's oldest surviving buildings. It was built in 1746 by Nathan Wilbur, a Nantucket sailor, who had seen windmills in Holland. Nathan's neighbors ridiculed his idea but he went ahead on his own to design and build the 50-foot windmill, using oaken beams taken from shipwrecks held together with hickory pins driven by a wooden mallet. The arms were built 30 feet long and six feet wide. When the mill was in operation, they were covered with sailcloth lashed into place with tarred cord run through eyelets. A spruce mast, 50 feet long by a foot wide, was fitted into the upper end into the movable top, the lower end into the hub of a wheel on the ground which enabled the top to be turned so the sails would face the wind.

It was a target hard to miss, and during the Revolutionary War a British cannonball hit the east wall and passed through the structure, barely missing the miller.

The Mill had a number of owners over the years. For a long time it belonged to the Swain family until in 1828 it had become so rundown that Nathan Swain sold it to Jared Gardner for firewood for the sum of 20 dollars. The shrewd Gardner, a millwright, did not burn his mill, but put it back into working order and eventually sold it again at a good profit. It ran again for a number of years until the last bag of meal was

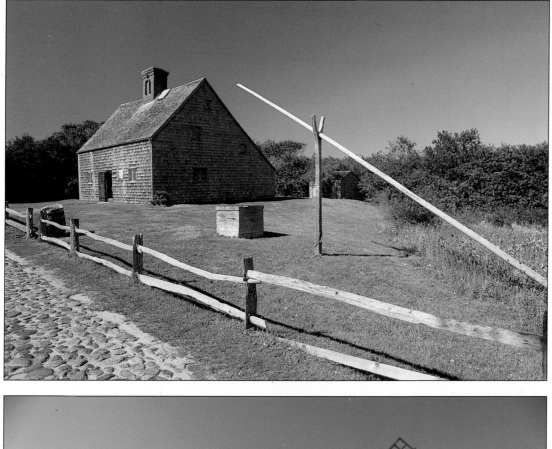

Nantucket's 'Oldest House' **above** was built in 1686 for Jethro Coffin and his bride, Mary Gardner. The marriage healed a breach between two prominent early island families.

Nantucket's Old Mill **left below**, dating back to 1746, holds a special place in the affections of residents. When needed repairs caused the mill to shut down, its restoration to working order in 1977 was cause for an island-wide champagne celebration.

ground in 1892 and the mill shut down for good. In 1897, it was bought at auction for 885 dollars by Miss Caroline French of Boston, who presented it to the Nantucket Historical Association to be preserved as a bit of island history. A tablet inside the door marks her gift.

As a sentimental landmark, the Mill holds a special place in the affections of the island. A number of old-time Nantucketers have held the post of custodian over the years to ensure its care. The most recent problem developed in 1976, when the drive shaft developed dry rot. A white oak pole 18 inches square by 20 feet long was needed as a replacement, and a huge tree was trucked from Ohio to do the job. Over a ton of wood chips had to be whittled away before the new shaft could be fitted into place. When the mill resumed grinding corn on July 27, 1977, the event was marked on the island with a champagne celebration.

Other Landmarks

Nantucket churches are other important local landmarks. The Unitarian Church, built in 1809, was the original town watchtower where, for over 100 years, two night watchmen stood guard, ready to sound the alarm if fire broke out. The tower was also used to sight the "house flags" of returning ships, good news that spread quickly to the sailors' families. The first town clock was placed in the tower in 1823, following installation of a bell in 1815. The bell has rung three times daily every day for over 150 years.

The Congregational Church on Centre Street is known for its *trompe l'oeil* painting and huge brass chandelier, and the spectacular view of the town from its tower. The church is on a high point called Beacon Hill in the early days because beacons were burned here to help ships reach port safely. The first bell tower was here; the bell was made by Paul Revere. St. Paul's Episcopal Church, a replacement for the original church lost in an 1846 fire, is noted for its Tiffany windows.

There are three Nantucket museums in town. The Whaling Museum on Broad Street contains memorabilia of the island's best known industry in an 1847 building that was once a candle factory. The exhibits include a jawbone of a whale that stands two stories high, a vivid reminder of the skill and strength required to capture such creatures. The Peter Foulger Museum next door collects the treasures of the early days—antique farming tools, oil paintings, lightship baskets, Oriental rugs and fine porcelain from the China trade to name a few. The member of the Folger family who established the museum asked that the old spelling of the name be retained.

A different side of island life is exhibited at the Fair Street Museum. Artists like John Singleton Copley, Gilbert Stuart and Tony Sarg all visited and painted Nantucket. This museum preserves their work and the canvasses and watercolors of many island artists. The sea views and landscapes that inspired them can be seen on a visit to the rural Nantucket away from the center of town.

Around the Islands

The elbow-shaped island of Nantucket is 14 miles long by 7 miles wide, with the historic town located on the northern side at the entrance to the large protected harbor.

The rest of Nantucket Island is a world apart, low irregular hills sometimes ending in steep sand bluffs above the Atlantic. On the island are thickets of scrub oak and pine, mealy-plum and bayberry, kettle ponds, cranberry bogs, swamplands where lush stands of wild grapes and blueberries grow and the most vast expanse of open heath to be seen outside of Scotland, a scene reminiscent of some of the English moors.

Like all of the outlands, Nantucket still bears the imprint of the glacier. Its hills are the moraine deposits, the moors are the outwash plains left when warming trends created streams that carried crushed rock and gravel sloping to the ocean shore. Hummock and Long Ponds were once melting streams that

Nantucket's high and handsome Gothic First Congregational Church **opposite** was built with whaling money in 1834. Also known as the Old North Church, it offers a tower view that is a living map of the island and its cobbled lanes and cupolas, moors, hills, ponds and beaches.

Previous pages and **center** Nantucket's outer island is an other-worldly landscape of ponds, moors and heath, dwarf trees and thickets where birds and animals find shelter and cranberry bogs that form a magic carpet of color in autumn.

flowed across the plains to the sea, later walled off by the ocean with dams of sand. Other kettle ponds on the island are the result of stubborn chunks of ice that remained when the glacier began to recede.

Winds, storms and tides have also altered the island landscape. The weather station on Nantucket has recorded winds up to 91 miles per hour. The winds in combination with salty soil prevent tall trees from growing on much of the island.

. The winds and pounding surf also continually eat at the bluffs on the island and make the perch of some of its lighthouses precarious. Sankaty Light is one currently threatened by severe erosion, and a 1984 nor'easter took down the Great Point Lighthouse built in 1818. The Coast Guard went to work immediately on a replacement.

Great Point itself became an island after the storm until the winds and tides moved the sand enough to re-form a connection to the mainland. Tuckernuck, a tiny island off the western side of Nantucket, was once the northwest tip of the island until erosion slowly wore away the bridge of land connecting it. A storm in 1896 permanently severed the two bodies of land, as nature continued to rearrange her island kingdoms. Esther Island, originally known as Old Smith Point, suffered the same fate in 1971.

The Great Lighthouse on the north end of the island was visible 14 miles to sea as a beacon to warn sailors of the treacherous Great Point Rip, shoals and currents that were the scene of 43 shipwrecks between 1863 and 1890. In 1899, a red sector in the light was inserted to mark Cross Rip Shoal and the other shoals south of it and wrecks became less common.

Beaches and Bogs

Nantucket's beaches are her glory for most visitors to the island. You come to beach no matter which direction you choose—calm and peaceful on the north, rough and tumble to the

south. The Jettie and Dionis both face Nantucket Sound, offering views of billowing sails and busy mainland ferries. These are town-run beaches popular for swimming, snorkeling, sunbathing and shell-gathering. Dionis, further out of town, offers miles of sandy dunes to provide shelter and privacy. A walk down the beach to peaceful Eel Point is a restful and scenic sojourn.

Southern shore beaches such as Siasconset, Nobadeer, Cisco and Madaket are challenging, especially after a storm. Even on balmy days, the waves can be high on these surf beaches, and only strong swimmers are advised to tackle the undertow. However, for beach walkers these are favorite spots, as are the many secluded out-island ocean beaches, where the only company is likely to be gulls and the sea. Surfside on the south shore is one of the islands most popular beaches, and the

Sankaty Head Lighthouse
sheds a beacon that can be seen 29 miles out
to sea. Its historic site atop
sandy cliffs is threatened by erosion from the
ever-constant pounding
waves.

Right Many of the quaint summer cottages along 'Sconset's lanes were originally fishermen's shanties built in the seventeenth and eighteenth centuries, and bear traces of a building style dating back to medieval Wales. Some are made of wood rescued from shipwrecks.

American Sycamore This magnificent tree, found in moist areas throughout the east, is the tallest broad-leaf tree species in the United States.

stretch between it and Cisco, known as Mia-comet, is a secluded area favored by those who like to do their sunning in the buff.

The ultimate faraway stretch of beach is Great Point off Wauwinet, the lighthouse site that can be reached by boat or beach hike over untouched white sand.

Nantucket's bogs, another prominent feature of the landscape, developed when moss and sedges formed coverings over a pond, cutting off oxygen and causing peat to grow underneath. Peat was the principal fuel on the island until "modern" coal stoves were introduced.

Cranberry vines easily take root in the top layers of moss, creating wild bogs all over Cape Cod and the Islands that have been cultivated by enterprising residents. Nantucket currently boasts one of the largest cranberry bogs in the world. The bogs and the fields of heather create a rosy glow that covers almost

the entire outer island in the fall.

Over many years, as bogs begin to dry out, shrubs take root and swamp trees such as red maples, white cedars and black gums follow. These changes turning bogs to dry land also can be seen in all of their stages on Nantucket. The ancient pond beds where soil has been enriched by decaying plants grow the island's largest trees, creating forests that will grow as high as the protection afforded by the sheltering hills around them. Ferns and woodland wildflowers grow in the damp soil in the shade of the trees.

An excellent way to see the variety of the Nantucket landscape is by bicycle. Two of the prime areas to be explored are Siasconset and Wauwinet, tiny settlements that still miraculously match one eighteenth-century visitor's description: "Perfectly unconnected with the real world and far removed from its perturbations."

Above The village of 'Sconset is a unique world unto itself. Small fisherman's cottages comingle with the summer homes of the rich.

Below Away from the tourists and excitements of Nantucket Town, 'Sconset is for those who love the sea and peace and quiet.

Right The miniature cottages of 'Sconset, nicknamed the "patchwork village".

Sconset

The better known of the two, Siasconset, universally referred to as 'Sconset, is a beguiling village set between the cranberry bogs and the rose-covered bluffs overlooking the Atlantic. The miniature cottages winding along 'Sconset's narrow lanes are among the island's oldest, dating back to its seventeenth- and eighteenth-century origins as a whaling outpost. They are fishermen's shanties altered and added to over the years, and in their scale and style are reminiscent of a building style that goes back to medieval Wales. Many are made more unique because they were built with used wood brought from town or rescued from shipwrecks, accounting for 'Sconset's old nickname of "Patchwork Village."

The special flavor of the village began to attract visitors. By the late 1800s, when the Nantucket Central Railroad extended its tracks to provide a 35-minute connection from town, trains like the Dionis and 'Sconset were carrying passengers who included many of the luminaries of the American stage, stars like Lillian Russell and Joseph Jefferson, who came to vacation in what had become a summer haven for Broadway stars.

Eventually the actors' colony declined and 'Sconset was left as a peaceful village, containing a handful of shops and the island's best-known gourmet restaurant. There are one or two inns, but because there are few lodgings for transients, most summer people own or rent houses here, helping the village retain its peaceful air and uncrowded beaches. The antique water pump that once served the entire community at a central wooden well remains in the center of the village as a reminder of the past.

One other bit of history has disappeared. Marconi established a wireless station in 'Sconset that was the first to report maritime news or transmit calls for help at sea. Sankaty Head lighthouse, a beacon to ships for many years, remains near 'Sconset on the cliffs that George Weymouth described in 1604.

The effects of erosion can be seen not only at Sankaty but by following right at the rotary in 'Sconset to the road along the Atlantic to the Coast Guard Station and Tom Nevers Head, a wild and scenic spot where wind and water is said to be taking up to nine acres a year.

Wauwinet

Wauwinet, named for one of the Indian Sachems on the island, is less developed than 'Sconset. It consists of miles of ocean and bay-front beach to tempt strollers, sunworshippers and fishermen, a few houses and one hotel. The water pump here still serves the entire community, and when it shuts down from November to May, the residents must move elsewhere.

Wauwinet drew growing numbers of fishermen attracted by the strand of land dubbed "the haulaway," a strip separating the calm inner harbor from the open Atlantic where dories could literally be hauled from one body of water to the other.

As in 'Sconset, the fishermen built huts here that were expanded over the years, but this community soon centered on Wauwinet House, a rambling gray-shingled beachhouse opened by James Backus in 1897 to serve meals for fishermen on its big screened porch. Until the 1940s, a catboat made the trip from Nantucket town to Backus' pier twice a day, bringing visitors who wanted an outing and a 50-cent lobster dinner. When the guests began asking to stay overnight, Wauwinet turned into a thriving summer hotel. The hotel remains, as does the natural beauty, preserved by the Backus' gift of more than 500 acres of surrounding land to the Massachusetts Trustees of Preservation, a conservation group. A four-mile curved stretch of sand leads to Great Point and the lighthouse site, a solitary and stunning beach walk.

A Fragile Treasure

On Nantucket the breezes still roll across the moors and rustle through the sea grass. But, vulnerable to wind and sea and the intrusions of unthinking developers, Nantucket treads a fine line between accommodating the many visitors who want to enjoy her pleasures and maintaining the character and beauty that accounts for her appeal. In 1984, the Nantucket Land Bank, a project designed to impose a tax on all land transactions, was overwhelmingly voted in by island residents. Its proceeds are earmarked to buy up property for public use.

The Nantucket Historical Association, which owns 12 historic buildings and the Lighthouse Ship, and the Conservation Foundation, responsible for the maintenance of over 40 properties, are other strong forces to preserve the island's architecture and save its marshes and moors from being overrun. The Conservation Foundation was founded in 1965 to protect the island for future generations. To date, it has set aside through gift and purchase more than 4,200 of the island's 31,600 acres. Among its major acquisitions are some eight miles of public beach at Coatue, Madaket, Eel Point, Dionis, Squam, South Shore, Cisco and Head of the Plains.

But the conservationists have their work cut out for them. At the present rate of building, 100 to 120 new homes per year, the island must absorb 1,200 homes in the next decade alone, a growth rate that could devastate its physical appearance.

"The little gray lady of the sea" with her cobblestones, weathered seaman's cottages and captains' mansions, her bountiful beaches, marshes and moors and wide-open spaces, is unique in New England and in the nation.

American Oystercatcher This long-legged red-beaked bird can be seen wading in shallow water looking for mollusks and crabs.

Overleaf A typical 'Cape Cod' style house in 'Sconset. The coloring and structural details are much as they were in Colonial times.

CONCLUSION

hat is Cape Cod? It is a narrow stretch of land jutting into the fathomless sea and so far man has not been able to devastate it so it is as beautiful as young love's fragile dreaming."

Cape Cod's resident writer, Gladys Taber, who wrote these words in 1971, is gone now, as is some of the open landscape she loved. But in spite of the growth that has come with passing years, much of the fragile and remarkable beauty of the Cape and its islands remains—at least for now.

America's development began on Cape Cod, with the Pilgrim fathers who made their way across a perilous sea to find a better life. As the civilization they helped to create grows ever busier and more complex, the need becomes more pressing to escape back to the beginnings, to a place where we can still live with nature and learn our place in the scheme of things.

The simple and proud Cape Cod cottage, along with the wooden fishing boats in the harbors, take us back to our beginnings and a time when Americans made a life by making the most of the opportunities nature provided. The windmills and wharves, the fine homes built by merchants and sea captains, bear witness to the enterprise and bravery of the men who found prosperity in an uncharted land where they faced the challenge of mapping a course so those who came after could follow.

The sea that helped sustain them still offers us sustenance. We no longer must depend on the fruits of the sea to survive, as our ancestors did, but the chance to gaze at an unspoiled seascape, to walk by the shore and be soothed by the sound of waves is nourishment for the soul that we still crave.

The restless ocean, the still and shimmering ponds, the woodlands, the open moors, the songs of birds are healing respites that allow us to find ourselves, to return to that other world of concrete replenished and refreshed.

With care they will remain for generations to come . . . Cape Cod, Martha's Vineyard, Nantucket . . . silver-shingled cottages, white blossoms of beach plums in springtime, cranberry bogs and heathery moors in fall, golden beaches, blue skies and blue seas of summer . . . timeless pleasures, waiting to welcome us back as seasons pass and years go gracefully by.

It is up to us—all of us who love the sounds and sights of the sea—to care for and preserve these fragile outer lands from overdevelopment, to save the very beauty that crowds come here to seek. They depend on us for survival, these glorious places by the sea, and in our over-civilized world we depend upon them as well.

For as Gladys Taber said so well: "The sea herself is an eternal reminder of how small man is and how good a wide horizon."

Opposite Tombstone from the Federated Church, Edgartown. Most of these headstones were erected in the memory of sailors lost

at sea.

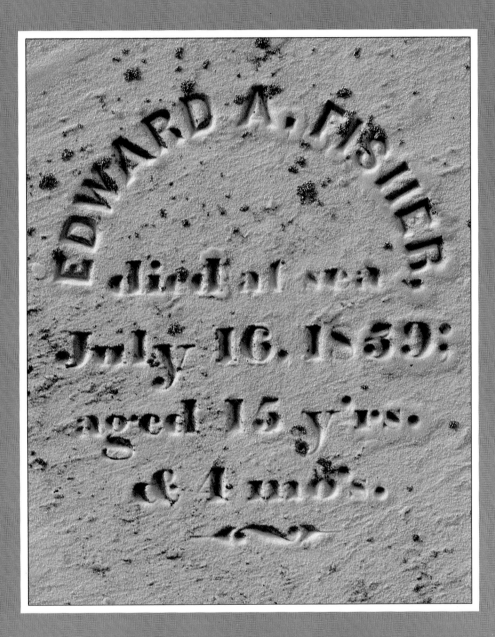

INDEX

PICTURE CREDITS

Leonard Harris: pp.13, 14, 15, 16, 17, 18/19 (left, bottom), 26, 32/33, 35, 36 (top right), 37, 38, 39, 41, 42, 43, 44 (bottom), 46 (bottom right), 47, 52, 53, 54/55, 61, 65 (top left), 68/69, 72/73 (left, centre), 76 (bottom left, top right, centre), 80 (top), 84/85, 86 (bottom), 133

Ian Howes: pp.6, 9, 11, 18/19 (top), 20/21, 22/23, 24/25, 27, 28, 29, 30, 31, 36 (top left, bottom left, bottom centre,

bottom right), 40, 44 (top), 45, 46 (top, bottom left), 47, 48, 49, 50, 51, 56, 57, 58/59, 6062/63, 64, 65 (top right, bottom centre), 66, 67, 70/71, 73 (right), 74/75, 76 (top left), 79, 80 (left, bottom), 82/83, 86 (top left, centre, right), 87, 88, 89, 94, 95, 96/97, 98, 99, 100/101, 102, 103, 104, 105, 106/107, 108, 109, 110, 111, 112, 113, 114/115, 116, 117, 118, 119, 120, 121, 122/123, 128/129, 132, 134/135, 140 (top right), 144 (bottom) 145, 146, 147, 149, 150, 151, 152/153, 154, 155, 156, 157 (top),

158, 160/161, 162/163, 164, 165, 166, 167, 268, 170

Eunice Harris: p.12

Peter Ralston: pp.93, 124, 125, 126/127, 130, 138, 139, 140 (centre), 140/141 (bottom), 141 (top left, centre), 142/143, 144 (top), 148, 149, 157 (bottom)